SUNDAY ADELAJA

WHO AM I?

WHY AM I HERE?

HOW TO DISCOVER YOUR PURPOSE AND CALLING IN LIFE

Sunday Adelaja
Who Am I? Why Am I Here?
©2016 Sunday Adelaja
ISBN 978-1-908040-46-6

Interior & Cover design by Alexander Bondaruk

CONTENTS

INTRODUCTION TO THE ENGLISH EDITION

Dear readers, this book "Who am I? Why am I Here?" was originally written by me in Russian language, being the language in which I have written over 200 of my books. However due to numerous requests and appeals from English speaking people all over the world, I decided to translate this book to English.

You will of course understand why I could not sit down once again to start writing the same book all over in a different language. I had no time, I had to write new ones. The reason I'm telling you this story is for you to bear with us if you find some imperfections in the language of this book. It is always a difficult task to translate books from one language to the other. Several people worked on it just for the English people to be able to discover the germ in this book, to them I owe my appreciation. I hope the value and content of this book will compensate for all the imperfection in its delivery. It is my prayer that as you read this book, God will speak to some of you to help us both to perfect the language of this book and in editing some other books that we are trying to print in the English language.

If you are a professional writer, we will appreciate your efforts as well in rewriting some of these books into better English language once it has been roughly translated from Russian language. The biggest benefit of the book is however the blessing to discover who you really are. This book will help you to do just that. You will find out who you are, you will discover your calling and the purpose of your calling on the earth. May the Lord bless you as you read.

From the author.

Sunday Adelaja

INTRODUCTION

A cemetery is a literal gold mine of the richest ideas, the perfect business projects, the greatest discoveries, the most astounding musical scores and dynamic masterpieces of literature, theatre and peace treaties — all of them unheard in this world; all buried with the one created to accomplish them. "Why?" you ask. They are buried with people who were to make their own contributions to the development of mankind, medicine, science, culture and government. People are born to change the world. There are people who failed to step forward and believe in the dream that was living within them. There are people who did not discover their destiny. People who failed to hear that inner voice that builds dreams and visions of greatness.

Unfortunately, all these wonderful dreams, ideas and projects are now buried with their authors. They will never be brought to life because they were given to people born on planet Earth for a specific purpose and a specific time. But *YOU* still have a chance! You are still alive! The voice of our Creator's heart and the cry of the Universe calls:

"Human being! Do not make light of your life. Do not live it running the rat race. You need to take advantage of the opportunity to become the kind of person that you have been created to be. Find yourself and fulfil your mission!"

Just look around you of those alive right now:

- 29% will die of cardiovascular diseases.
- 20% will die of cancer.
- 10% or more will die of AIDS.

- 9.6% will die of apoplectic attack.
- 1.5% will commit suicide.
- 0.6% will drown.
- 0.5% will perish in fires.
- 0.09% will die of Hepatitis C.

However, candidly speaking, we all will die of something, BUT 99% of the people will die with their mission unfulfilled.

What is the one thing you should really fear?

PRACTICAL SUGGESTIONS FOR READING THIS BOOK

This book can change your life!

Often, when reading an inspiring or instructional book, we decide to apply the lessons we have learned. However, sadly, just as often, after only a few weeks, due to the business of life, we slowly forgot about our intentions. The fact is, you can have a lot of diverse and useful knowledge in your head, but if you don't follow through and use it you will never reap the benefits. Much of what you will read here will not be anything new to you, the question is what will you do with what you read here?

Here are six practical steps, that will help empower you to turn your good intentions into good actions:

1. Read this book several times

While reading the truths contained here, pause often to ponder what is being shared. Ask yourself how and when you can practically implement what is recommended in your life. After you have finished a detailed study of the book, re-read it every month as a refresher and a reminder of the truths you have learned. Let this book become a handbook in your tool chest for success.

2. Read out loud

It has been proven that reading out loud helps you to more effectively connect with the truth you are reading, which in turn empowers you to release into your life the power that is contained in every word. It is imperative that you not only see the words, but also that you hear every word. Jesus said, *"If anyone has ears to hear, let him hear."* And He said to them, *"Pay attention to what you hear: with the measure you use, it will be measured to you, and still more will be added to you. For to the one who has, more will be given, and from the one who has not, even what he has will be taken away."* (Mark 4:23–25, Emphasis added). Jesus wasn't primarily saying be careful what you hear others say, (though that is vitally important) — what He was emphasizing was the importance of what you hear yourself saying. Why? Because you will believe what you hear yourself saying! Spoken words have a 'wave like' nature and when they are spoken (and heard), they have a dynamic effect on everything around them. Words are important. Do not neglect the power of Spirit-filled spoken words! Do not let the life-transforming power of your spoken words lay untapped and unused!

3. Underline and take notes

This isn't fiction, it isn't a novel. While reading this book, keep a pen or highlighter nearby. As you read, the truths contained herein will leap out at you. Capture those truths by underlining key words, sentences and paragraphs. This simple action will significantly increase the impact they will have on you and will enhance your ability to remember them. Also, take the time to record your thoughts and notes in the margins — make this book 'your' book. Underlining not only makes reading the book more interesting, but it also is helpful when you return regularly to review it again.

4. Re-read the underlined portions

As you are impacted by the truths contained here and underline them, it makes it easier to quickly review the most important and personally applicable truths in this book. As I stated earlier, in order to get the best results from reading this book, you should review it often.

I encourage you to allow the truths you have marked inspire you to improve your life. I am amazed at our ability, as human beings, with the power we have to remember things. I am just as amazed at our ability to forget. That is why we must do everything we can to help capture the truths we so desperately need so we can both review and apply these truths to our life.

5.   Immediately apply the principles learned

The best way to benefit from the truths you will be learning is to consciously apply what you have heard and learned in your life's circumstances. You see, I can teach you, but I can't make you learn. Only you can make that choice. Teaching is a dynamic two-way process. The most effective way to learn is when we put into practice what we have been taught. As you read this book, if you want to master the principles contained here, put them into practice at every opportunity until they are second nature. If you do not practice them, if you do not choose to live them, the sad fact is that you will very quickly forget them. Only that which is recognized as important and of value and put into practice remains in the memory.

6.   Set realistic priorities for applying what you learn

Don't try to conquer the whole world at once. You must walk before you run. Instead of trying to do everything you will be learning in this book at once, start by selecting one to three points and begin to apply them in your life until they become second nature. You will only receive the optimal benefit from the truths contained here as you apply them by constant repetition.

At the end of each chapter, you will find golden nuggets which will summarize the most important ideas shared throughout the chapter. To further help cement the truths you will be learning, I have also included self-assessment quizzes designed to help you synergize what you have learned. I have also included practical exercises that will help you implement them and make them an integral part of your lifestyle. They are not designed just for reading. Please read that last sentence again. If you desire to get the maximum results and benefits from these practical exercises, I strongly advise you to start applying them immediately, otherwise, the cares and worries of life will distract you. If you allow that to happen, they will keep you from achieving your destiny and the transformation you desire in your life will not occur.

In my years of sharing these life changing truths with multitudes of people, I have noticed that the difference between those who do and do not succeed, is that those who do succeed do what they know to do. Those who do not succeed usually fail because they do not do what they know to do, or if they do, they do so in a 'superficial' manner.

Life isn't a game — it is for real. It is made up of real choices that have real consequences, for the choices we make. How you approach and engage with the truths in this book; how you study, using the tools provided and how faithfully you apply them to your life's circumstances will be the deciding factor on how much benefit and receive and also how successful you become. Therefore, I ask you to take the exercises seriously, as they are not for the benefit of the author, but rather, because I desire to empower and equip you to succeed. The most effective way to approach the exercises is to get away to a quiet place where you will not be disturbed, perhaps at a time when there is no one else at home, or early in the morning before anyone else is up, or late at night when everyone else is asleep, so you don't have to be concerned about being interrupted.

As you work through the book and the materials, make sure you 'look back' and meditate on the previous chapter(s) and on all the points that you have underlined and highlighted. Reflect on your decisions and write down your follow-up. Don't forget to schedule specific times for your time of study. This will help you stay focused on taking the necessary steps needed to transform your life indefinitely. Share the book and what you have learned with someone else — a study partner — so you have someone to be accountable to, who can partner with you as you work through the book.

Write down the date and time you start on your new journey. Let this date be the starting point for a new beginning in your life!

GUIDELINES FOR THE IMPLEMENTATION OF PRACTICAL TASKS

1. *CAUTION: These tasks are not just to be read, they are VERY IM-PORTANT. From my years of sharing these truths with people, I know from experience, how often people 'superficially' perform such tasks. Don't be guilty of making that mistake — this is for you, take them seriously.*

2. *For optimum results, I suggest you start applying what you learn immediately, otherwise, you run the risk of delaying your success.*

3. *Find a quiet place and answer all the questions.*

4. *Meditate on the previous chapter, on everything that you underlined or highlighted, reflect on them and make sure you write out your steps of action.*

5. *Set yourself a time frame. Do not postpone your new beginnings.*

6. *Find a study partner — someone to whom you can be accountable to, who can remind you about your goals.*

HOW TO TAKE THE SELF-ASSESSMENTS

The self-assessments that follow each chapter are designed to help you check your progress and determine where you are. Recognizing the areas where you need improvement is the first step in knowing where, and how, to apply the principles presented in this book. Respond thoughtfully and honestly to the self-assessments.

For each self-assessment item, there should only be one response. Next to each possible answer you will see a number in brackets denoting the value of that response. Your totaled score will indicate how ready you are to live out the principles in question. The self-assessments are designed only to help you discover your areas that need improvement, not to humiliate you. Remember, we are all a work in progress and we all have areas we can improve in.

If you would like to get some psychological counselling or to participate in our practical training, designed to help facilitate the changes you desire in your life, you can use the following link to register: **http://www.universityoflife.com.** On this site you will also find many useful resources which will help you to build a successful life. Do not miss out on your opportunity to achieve your destiny!

PART 1

FIVE ESSENTIAL QUESTIONS OF HUMANITY

CHAPTER 1

WHO AM I?

WHO AM I?

"That moment I understood who I missed. I understood what person I lacked. I clearly realized who I longed for, who I missed for a long time and who I lacked every day I lived. I missed myself, True and Happy."

"What do you consider to be the most disgusting thing in the world?" is the question the young journalist was posing to travelers going through Kennedy Airport (USA) the morning of his greatest life changing encounter. There were many answers, all reflecting the devastating conditions of the world climate. Yet, when he saw a young Zen Monk in complete Buddhist dress, the journalist knew this would be a different viewpoint. With eagerness, he awaited the monk's answer to the question. The monk answered with a counter-question: "Who are you?" startled, the reporter answered, "I am John Smith" "No, that is just your name, but who are you?" "I am a journalist for a television company" "No, that is just your job, but who are you?" "I am a human being," "No, that is just your species, but who are YOU?" The journalist finally understood what the monk meant and stood there with his mouth wide open because he couldn't find anything to say. He really had never thought about "who HE was".

The monk then remarked: "That's the most disgusting thing in the world — being unaware of who you are."

Discovering your identity is the key to fulfilling your destiny.

If we are not aware of who we are, how will we know where we are going or how we should get there. Allow me to share another story that illustrates the necessity of understanding who you are.

A woman moved slowly along the snow-covered avenue of a city park. Snow was falling softly to the ground like a fluffy white bedspread. Serena has just turned 50. She had always lived what she thought was a successful, fulfilled life until in one swift blow, life had dealt her a bad hand and now she had nothing to live for.

Since she was 16, she knew that the one thing important to her was to have a nice home, a wonderful husband and be a good mother. She had done all of that and now it was all gone.

Her husband had come home from the office and had started a fight. They had both said some very bitter things which led to him walking out. He told her he was not returning home and had filed for a divorce.

Serena was left alone in a large luxury apartment without any means of financial support. She found herself alone, unemployed, without a family and without a way to make a living. She had devoted all of her life to her family. She had found meaning and purpose in her life by providing a clean and neat home, being a good mother and a wife. Now what was she to do?

Her heart was empty of purpose. She pictured herself having a different end to her life. A happy family was her main goal; her only goal; her only reason for living. She loved her husband despite all the problems in their relationship. She had made every effort to keep their family together. Serena was walking along the snow-covered avenue, grieving because she felt she had come to the end of her life. Her dreams were not coming true. She had achieved her goal: she had had a family, a husband and children. Now she was alone with nothing. She felt unwanted and lonely. She did not understand why she should continue to live.

Serena began to ask herself serious questions. She had achieved one goal, but that one goal was not enough. Circumstances forced Serena into a crisis of existence. Why live any longer? That small quiet voice inside began to question: "Who are you?" "Why were you created?" Each question led Serena to many more soul searching questions.

Who am I? Am I a housewife? Am I an ex-wife? Am I the mother of two children? Why did I come into this world? Is this all there is to life, to marry and give birth to children or are there other purposes for my existence? If there are other purposes, how can I know what they are.

She decided to begin training sessions for self-development where she was encouraged to set and achieve goals. These well-known speakers said that aimless life leads to depression. They taught her the importance of goals and how to attain these goals. Still, she wasn't satisfied. She wondered, "Is there any difference if the purpose of my whole life is to create a business or to create a family? What if I set a goal of having a successful business — and then lose it?" She wondered if she would face the same dismal end. After all, what was her real purpose? Suddenly, Serena understood clearly that she had to find herself. She had to identify herself and who she was in this world. That needed to come first. Only then could she start looking for her purpose in life.

> *"The greatest tragedy in a human life is not death, but life without purpose."* (MYLES MUNROE)

Unfortunately, a lot of people in the world live almost unconsciously. They live as if they are in a dream. They get up every morning, brush their teeth, get dressed, go to work or to school and direct their businesses. They are incessantly doing this and that. They seldom think about the purpose they were uniquely designed to fulfil and don't ask themselves the question of who they are or what their identity is.

In our dynamic age, the speed of motion is increasing. The problems that need to be solved are growing in number and the business of life is overpowering. Very little time is given to how we should think about essential matters, such as how to support our life and the life of our family and children.

A person who is in a constant rat race seldom has time to think whether or not he is living his life properly. He doesn't take the time to ponder who he is and why he was born into this world until something serious happens to make him abandon his "essential" activity. Then he starts to think about the philosophical questions, what humanity has been trying to answer during all of its existence on planet Earth.

Who am I? Why did I come into this world? What am I living for? What is the purpose of my life? Where did I come from? What does it mean "to be oneself"? Where is my place in this life? Why was I born on this planet?

Every human being asks these questions of himself. If we want to live consciously, if we want to enjoy our life and not spend it simply completing the task of surviving, each of us must find answers to the questions concerning our destiny.

The life of a man who is ignorant of his destiny is meaningless.

Today we can come across millions of people like Serena. They are busy creating families, building businesses, working from morning until night, but they don't know what it is to live a full life.

The life of people who do not know their destiny becomes an infinite chain of activities that in fact do not actually mean anything for their success. We can compare a life without a goal to an equestrian on an obstinate horse: much movement but little headway.

You are created with a purpose. This is the reason you were born. That is why it is necessary to understand your destiny: when you realize your purpose it brings understanding deep within you.

Consider a cell phone. It was produced for a definite purpose; each phone has its own special features. The characteristics of iPad differ from the characteristics of a cell phone. Each of us also has our own unique traits and we need them to fulfill our destiny.

You were born on this planet with a definite purpose and the entire world is in need of the gift you have. The world is in need of the unique purpose you were created for. If you do not find yourself and your purpose, the world will be worse for it. For example, what would the world be like, if Steve Jobs did not invent the first Macintosh? What if we didn't have the iPad or iPhone? What if Edison did not invent the electric light bulb that later appeared in all of our houses? The world will lose something if you do not find yourself, if you don't answer the question "Who am I?"

If you do not carry out your mission, the world will lose what God created you to do and your gift to the world will be buried with the other riches in that cemetery we described at the beginning of this book. Do you want to lead an unfulfilled, wasted life or do you want to be all you were created to be?

WHO AM I?

This first question is the most important and difficult. You will be someone else if you do not answer this question. Most people play the role that belongs to someone else; they pretend to be other people because they have never thought of their true selves.

We become the people who are made by our family and society when we are ignorant of who we are. We speak using generally accepted slang, we wear the latest fashions in clothes and we think in terms of common stereotypes. We live with the key purpose of receiving the approval of those around us because we don't know who we are in reality. Moreover, until you have answered the question: "Who am I?" you will not be capable of living your own life.

The question **"Who am I?"** is the first question that every person should ask himself. The answer must be considered with sound judgment. "Who am I?" is a complicated question. Most people have never answered it.

If you don't know who you are, you will be someone else. Most people turn out to be someone else. That is why we conceal our true selves and wear the image of others. We bear their brand. A company builds its success and becomes popular with its unique appearance and identity. This is their brand. If you don't have your own identity you will adopt the brand of another.

No one wants to be an imitation of another. When we speak, dress and think like others, we live with the goal of achieving the approval they have. We do this because we do not know who we are. Until you realize who you are, you will not be able to start living the life you are intended to live. That is why this lesson is the first and primary life lesson.

"He who once found himself cannot lose anything in this world. He who once understood the man in him can understand all humanity." (STEFAN ZWEIG, AN AUSTRIAN WRITER)

If a man realizes who he is, he cannot be hurt, humiliated or offended. He will not be envious of others or condemn them because he knows his own value, uniqueness and peculiar contribution. He will not react to the negative things surrounding him. He cannot lose his peace and gladness, because he lives at peace with himself. Even if he loses his finances or suffers a failure in his career, it will not touch his inner world and make him overly upset or nervous, because these will only be external circumstances. He is aware of his value. He is confident of his strength. He understands that if he must, he can start from the beginning and achieve success again.

"Nobody is as miserable as the man who longs to be somebody else other than the person he is, both physically and mentally." (ANGELO PATRI)

Immanuel Kant, a German philosopher and the founder of German classical philosophy said:

"A human being is 'the most essential object in our world'."

Existentialism is one of the most popular and influential trends of the contemporary social thought. For existentialists, "I" is represented as an active creative pole of consciousness. A human should realize himself and be responsible for himself if he wants to become the true person he is to be.

Jesus Christ gave the best answer to this philosophical question, "Who Am I?"

He said, *"I am..."* Jesus Christ used these words more frequently than any others: "I am the Bread of Life; I am the Word of Life; I am the Spirit of Truth; I am Life; I am the Good Pastor; I am the Door; I am the Resurrection."

Jesus Christ was aware of who He was. He knew the answer to the question "Who am I?" He knew His destiny and the purpose of His birth on this planet. This self-knowledge helped Jesus to be focused on His target from His early childhood. He was never distracted by the demands of His surroundings. He was never tempted to live by the standards of other people or to be guided by someone else's opinions. He was purposefully going towards His goal, to release humanity from its slavery to sin. The result is that Jesus Christ is the most outstanding Person who has ever lived on planet Earth. His heroic life is described in the Bible, translated into virtually all of the world's languages and has sold more copies than any book that was ever printed.

Getting to know who you are is the most essential information that you can find out about yourself. It is the secret to ensuring that your life will not be dull and unnoticed. The earlier you find the answer to this question, the more effective and successful a life you will be able to live.

Life stories of great and successful people help illustrate this principle.

Steve Jobs realized very early in life that his passion centered on computers. He answered the question "Who am I?" in the following way: "I am the man who wants to teach computers to think like people instead of teaching people to think like a computer." His life impacted the world and how we relate to computers. Steve Jobs went down in history as a pioneer and innovator. He changed history by creating the Apple II and the Macintosh. It's hard to imagine, a hippie without higher education from a small American town, comes to stand at the center of the world changer called "Apple." He is counted as the youngest multi-millionaire and the world has recognized him as a genius who turned his dreams into a new technical reality.

> *"Our time is limited, so do not waste it living someone else's life. Do not be trapped by dogmas — that means living by using other people's thoughts. Do not let the noise of other people's opinions muffle your own inner voice. The most important thing: have the courage to follow your heart and mind. Somehow, they already know what you really want to become. Everything else is of secondary importance."* (STEVE JOBS)

When answering the question "Who am I?" Bill Gates called himself the father of computer software. The knowledge and successful pursuit of his destiny made him the richest man in the world. From 1996 till 2007 and in 2009, he was nominated as the world's richest person according to the Forbes magazine. In the autumn of 2009, his wealth was estimated at $50 billion.

Being aware of who you are, you will ensure that you do not waste your time, spending energy on unnecessary things. That is the primary reason why, having focused on your target, you will be able to achieve more in your life than any ordinary person can ever do.

The most famous American President, Abraham Lincoln, considered that his destiny was to become the president of America, sweeping away slavery. On 1 January 1863, he boldly announced the Emancipation Proclamation declaring all slaves in the United States of America to be free. On 1 February 1865, Lincoln signed a joint Congressional Resolution introducing the 13th Amendment to the U.S. Constitution, which when ratified by the States, officially repealed slavery. It stated that "neither slavery nor involuntary servitude, except in cases of punishment when a guilty person was properly condemned for a crime that was committed, should not exist, either in the USA or in other places under its power."

The focus on his destiny and his understanding of his true self kept Abraham Lincoln from giving up after several failed attempts to become President.

When he was seven, his family was put out of the house for failure to pay the rent on time. He had to work hard in order to get food for himself and his family.

When he was nine, his mother died.

At the age of twenty-two, he lost his job as a shop messenger.

At twenty-three, he incurred a debt in order to become a partner at a small shop.

When he was twenty-six, his business partner died, leaving him with a tremendous debt that Lincoln spent many years paying back.

At the age of twenty-eight he proposed to his girlfriend with whom he had had a relationship for four years, but she refused marriage.

At the age of thirty-seven he was elected to the Congress after three failed attempts, but he was not re-elected two years later.

His four-year-old son died when Lincoln was forty-one.

At forty-five he made an attempt to get into the Senate, but he failed again. At the age of fifty-one he was elected to be the President of the United States.

How are you going to answer the question "Who am I?" Have you ever asked yourselves that question?

Your true "I", your spirit and your soul are, in fact free from social masks and the roles being imposed by your society. If you know who you are, it makes you immune to criticism; it reduces your fear of trials; you do not need to consider yourself to be worse or better than someone else.

If you know who you are, this knowledge will attract people in all types of situations and circumstances to support your intentions and ideas.

You can call for support from the ruler of the universe. Many understand that our life is not just our bones and body, that there is something more to life. They find they can accomplish what they were designed to be with God's help and guidance.

CHAPTER 2

MAKE YOUR NAME AND KNOW YOUR VALUE

MAKE YOUR NAME AND KNOW YOUR VALUE

WHO AM I?

To succeed and reach your life goals, you must answer this question. If when you think of yourself, you think only of your physical body — even if you are physically fit and firm, at your ideal weight with beautiful hair, eyes or lips — if that is how you gauge your success, you are mistaken. If you live long enough your hair will become gray, your body will become weak, so what then? Having an inaccurate or incomplete view of themselves is why many people are distressed with the process of aging.

In order not to be captured in a trap of depression at the latter end of your life, you should properly assess yourself, rightly understand your identity and realize that you are not the same as your appearance in the mirror. That person in the mirror is just the outside, your earth suit; the real you resides on the inside. Identifying someone by his, or her, outward appearance is often the first and most common error in the world.

What is the value of a human being? The value of human beings does not consist in their appearance. Some spend an hour a day on their makeup or hair, yet cannot find time for reading and self-development. Many are not engaged in any on-going self-education, gaining new knowledge, maturing their personality or improving their inner selves. It is all too common for people to invest time into appearances but not in developing their inner man. Remember, having a good head on our shoulders isn't just for decoration purposes!

Our head is designed to develop our intelligence, to devote ourselves to self-education, self-improvement and to broaden our perspective regarding the world around us; to broaden our capability of analyzing facts, events and to draw the right conclusions. Our head is there to facilitate our coming to an understanding of our purpose and setting the necessary goals to achieve that purpose.

Remember, you are God's unique creation. He didn't just create you to be a nice person and eat hamburgers until you die. No, He created you for His higher purpose and for your better good. A wise person understands this. In understanding and developing your true identity, you can stand on solid ground because you are a person of God's unique creation. This gives you intrinsic value and should impact your focus. Imitate the traits of your Creator. Develop your intellect and your creative ways of thinking.

You create a strong, unshakable internal core by understanding and pursuing the attributes that you want to inherit from your Creator. Your self-reliance, self-appraisal and self-perception depends on how successful you are at making these things your own.

MAKE YOUR NAME AND KNOW YOUR VALUE

Having already become a billionaire, Henry Ford arrived in England. At the visitor's office, he asked for the cheapest hotel in town. The office worker stared at him: Henry had a well-known appearance and newspapers from around the world often wrote about him. He stood in the visitor's office, wearing his coat which looked even older than its owner and requested information on the cheapest hotel in town. The worker asked with uncertainty: "If I am not mistaken, you must be Mr. Henry Ford? Doesn't your son always stay at the best hotels and isn't he always well-dressed? How can you ask for the cheapest hotel and wear a coat that seems to be as old as you? Do you really work to save your money?"

"I have no need to stay in a luxury hotel. Wherever I stay, I am still Henry Ford. Even in the cheapest Inn, I am still Henry Ford. My son is too young and inexperienced. He is afraid of what people may say, he is afraid they will judge him if he stays at a cheap hotel. As to this coat — yes — my dad used to wear it, but it does not matter. Why should I have to have new things? I am still Henry Ford whatever I am dressed in! I made my name and I know my value. I am Henry Ford, always and everywhere; all the other things do not really matter."

Henry Ford could afford to have any appearance that he wanted to have. He was aware of his true being. He formed an internal core identity which he lived out. He said: "I have made a name for myself and I know my value."

You see, if you do not know you have intrinsic value because of who you are and who you are meant to be, you will feel uncomfortable when you are not looking your best (in other's eyes) or if you are not wearing the latest fashion trend.

However, if you understand that you are not just your appearance or your physical body, you will be better equipped to handle negative feelings or imperfections regarding your outward appearance. Your inner knowledge of yourself is what matters. Developing a true and solid character and finding unique traits that belong only to you is a foundational thing.

"I made my name". What does this mean? It means that a man has successfully graduated through the process of internal self-development. He overcame the obstacles, hassles and roadblocks. He didn't stop just because the way was hard, rather, he found solutions to problems. He was continually engaged in educating himself, undertaking and fulfilling his responsibilities, and learned never to give up regardless of his circumstances. He developed the traits that are specific to successful people: passion — the ability to stay focused and the determination to never, never, never give up.

He developed endurance, steadfastness, perseverance and the will-to-win as the core parts of his character. He fought and won his inner battle against fears and restrictions (everyone has fear and inner battles — the difference between success and failure is how we process them). He wasn't concerned with conquering the world as much as he was dedicated to conquering himself and, therefore he made a name for himself. No one is born successful. Success requires preparation. Success comes from developing a strong inner character.

How did he manage to make a name for himself? It came from working hard, cultivating endurance and patience that even angels would love to have. Where many of us would stop and consider ourselves to have done enough to reach our purpose, he wasn't content and continued to move forward.

He overcame pain, weakness, laziness and ignorance. When people around him tried to tear him down, maybe they called into question his professionalism or even his physical attributes, maybe they tried to humiliate and falsely accuse him of things. Still, he did not allow these thoughts to flood his mind and cause him to focus on his shortcomings. Rather, he continued to believe in his abilities and strength. He believed the truth about himself, the truth that people are created to solve problems and overcome the limitations of their nature.

"When everything seems to be going against you, remember that the airplane takes off against the wind, not with it."

Perhaps, he did not take training courses on self-development, but learned from life by taking on responsibilities and constantly solving problems. He learned from the challenges and tasks required by his business. These things helped him create his internal character and develop the traits that led him to succeed. Thus he can claim that he has made a name for himself.

Let me ask you, what are you doing for your own self-development? What traits are you working on improving? Maybe you have never taken the time to think about it?

> "Thinking is the hardest work there is, which is probably the reason why so few engage in it." (HENRY FORD)

Don Marquis once said, "If you make people think they are thinking, they'll love you; but if you really make them think, they'll hate you".

I don't want you to hate me or even to not like me, but I am committed to helping you think and grow and succeed!

Each of us can improve our internal person and develop the character required for a successful life. We can do this in the same way that Henry Ford did it.

If you do not work on self-improvement or do not develop strength of character, you will be inclined to succumb to the opinions of the people surrounding you or to the standards criminally imposed on you by society.

People try to build their identity around external things such as appearance and clothes at the expense of neglecting the inner values of who they really are. Your main target should be to find and develop your own unique individuality and not let your focus be sidetracked and drift to external things.

> *"The main life objective of a human being is to give birth to himself and to become all that he has the potential to become — the person that he is supposed to be. The most outstanding outcome of this activity is the development of his own internal personality"* (ERICH FROMM, A GERMAN SOCIAL PSYCHOLOGIST AND PHILOSOPHER)

First of all, you should develop the "person" inside you; this means to pay attention and develop life within yourself. Only a person who has already developed life within himself will be able to extend a quality life to somebody else. That is why it is so necessary for everyone to develop their internal personality.

What was the life of well-known writer Paulo Coelho like — the life of the man who is quoted by presidents?

At the age of seven, he developed a desire to become a writer — his parents thought this a very strange desire. His mother advised him to first get a higher education in the engineering field and then write in his spare time.

"No, mum, I only want to be a writer, not an engineer who writes books".

His childhood dream came true almost 30 years later when he was 38. There were reasons for this.

In the beginning his parents dissuaded him from becoming a writer. They thought that a "real" profession like that of a lawyer or an engineer was more suitable for the conditions of the Brazilian garrison state of the 1960s. These types of careers could ensure a calm, quiet and successful life. Yielding to the pressure of his parents, Paulo entered the University of Rio de Janeiro and joined the Faculty of Law. This didn't last. Soon he gave up his studies.

His parents had no idea what to do with their determined and asocial son who they thought violated all generally accepted standards of behavior. His mother and father decided to send their son to a mental hospital.

So, at the age of 17 Paulo Coelho had convulsive shock therapy. He tried to escape from the clinic, but he was caught and returned. He made one more attempt and escaped.

He wandered around the country for some time and joined an amateur theatre. But he had to come back home because of a lack of money. He became a patient at the mental hospital again. In the end, Coelho underwent three courses of treatment. In 1974, Coelho and his wife were taken into custody. In prison, Coelho was tortured several times, and he confessed to having shown poor conduct. In order to save his life and be freed from prison, he focused on convincing people that he was crazy. He started to behave like a madman. He was found insane and set free.

It took Paulo Coelho years to rid himself of his dreadful memories of his past. In spite of being physically free, he felt shackled with the chain of fears that resulted from living behind bars.

His life's major turning point occurred when Coelho met a stranger in an Amsterdam cafe who told him to make the traditional Roman Catholic pilgrimage to Santiago de Compostela in Northern Spain. Coelho did so in 1986. As a result, he experienced an epiphany that readers of *The Alchemist* will recognize: he decided to follow his dream. Coelho set out to become a writer.

He explains that he has managed to conquer his fears and that he relies on the courage he has cultivated within himself. He finds it to be one of his major strengths.

That is what our self-development is all about: we conquer our fears and overcome our restrictions, conquer and recreate ourselves; we cultivate the traits that we need to achieve our life purpose, success and to carry out our mission.

STAY TRUE TO YOUR DREAM

Because he stayed true to his dream and of his awareness that he was created to write, Paulo Coelho pursued his career as a writer. The Brazilian writer's second novel "The Alchemist" came out in 1988.

This is the main idea of the book: "Achieving fulfillment to one's destiny is the only true obligation of a person." This is the lesson of life that Paulo Coelho reflected in his writing.

"There is only one thing that makes fulfillment of your dream impossible — the fear of failure," the writer argues in this book.

Immediately after it was published, the novel did not generate any special interest from the public. The initial sales did not even come near ten percent of expected sales.

With the help of his wife, Coelho sent copies of the book to influential people in Brazilian mass media. He gave interviews and presented lectures. Coelho was accepted by a large publishing house, Rocco. Their release of "The Alchemist" was a success. The book sold out immediately.

Soon Coelho made his way onto two bestseller lists: his novel "Diary of the Wizard" won the category "Non-Fiction" while "The Alchemist" won in the "Fiction" category.

Coelho kept pursuing his dream. He didn't give up with initial lack of success in selling his book. He personally put forth the effort to promote it. He knew its value and refused to accept its modest sales.

Coelho invested effort promoting his book, showing persistence and the will to win. He didn't have false modesty because he knew who he was. He was confident of his book being able to bring in much higher sales and recognition. He knew he was a great writer. If we know who we are and we have gone through a process of self- identification in accordance with the Creator's plan, we will no longer undervalue ourselves or be afraid. We will act.

Coelho did. Soon, a wave of success came! People bought one copy after another. He organized meetings through his own efforts and thousands came to the meetings. He took success into his own hand. He made sure that people knew the value of the book and that the demand for "The Alchemist" was not artificially created by the publishers.

Coelho became one of the favorite writers of our day because he sincerely talks to his readers and touches on topics that are important to them.

The secret behind his success is that he did not leave behind his childhood dream. He was not afraid to step out and become a writer even after years had passed and he was well into adulthood.

How many of us do not even have our own dream?

Most of us try to just live with what society tells us is important. We then live someone else's life, without trying to understand and become what we are really designed to be. Coelho's parents tried to make an engineer out of him. For the sake of their goal, they went so far as to send him to a mental hospital.

What an abyss of ignorance hiding under the guise of love and care!

If parents can treat a child like this, think of how society and our surroundings can pressure us to do what they want us to do and to be what they want us to be. Our task is not to yield. Our challenge is not to let life mold or break us. We need to know who we are and then stand strong.

It is up to you to set aside time for this book. It will help you identify yourself, your purpose and your destiny.

Dear reader, if you still find it difficult to answer the question "Who am I?" there are practical steps you can take: deepen your knowledge about your role in society; explore those things you do that are satisfying. Learn more about the character traits you have and those you want to develop. What is your passion? What makes you proud regarding your family roots? There are so many clues; this book will help you to find what the clues mean.

At the end of this chapter, you will find practical tasks. Don't make the mistake of overlooking them; completing them will help you to find the answers you need.

It is important for you to understand your purpose for living on planet Earth. If you haven't understood this yet, you really need to study the second part of this book. It is imperative! Complete all the practical tasks that are listed.

This is one of the main keys to understanding the purpose of your life; it is to ask yourself the question "What is an activity that I would do even if I am not paid?" If you would devote your time to an activity even if you didn't receive payment, you have found a key to your destiny.

If you know who you are and know that you live to achieve goals in keeping with who you are, it does not matter if people give you compliments or not. You can be satisfied in life because you have and are fulfilling your important mission in life.

YOU ARE NOT A BIOMASS

You were not born only to be like a bush or a tree, just to marry, reproduce and die. That is the existence of any plant or animal. You have a destiny. You are a human of intrinsic value. You were born to fulfill a mission. There is something you can do that nobody else can do.

You are the ONLY you there is. You have a purpose. You are not just a biomass. What is a biomass? A biomass is merely renewable organic material. You are far more than that.

You have a destiny. You were created in the image of God. When a human being is brought up with the concern of simply taking care of his body and the external aspects of his life, he is acting as though he is only a biomass. You are, or become, what you think you are. Until we begin to discover and create value, purposefully and systemically, we are not humans but only a biomass.

A human being living at the level of biomass will:

- wear attractive clothes;
- comply with the changing fashion and beauty standards;
- comply with all standards and patterns that are required by the surroundings and society.

Such a person will do whatever it takes to be accepted by the society — and live with a self-preservation instinct. A 'biomass' man lives by his instincts. He tries to look good on the outside. Inside, he is afraid to be himself. He is afraid of expressing his opinion and often avoids speaking in public. Such a man, perhaps because he has not been challenged or maybe because he is afraid, has not reflected deeply on his life. He has not come to terms with the fact that his actions are only a self-preservation instinct to survive in his environment and in society.

LIFE IN EVERYONE ELSE'S STYLE

A person living at this level of consciousness will react only to stimulus, e.g. to pleasure or pain. Again, his reaction comes from reflexes and instincts. He is not using logical, analytical thinking; he is not deeply analyzing things to draw meaningful conclusions. He repeats what he sees. For example, if he sees everyone going to work he will also do the same. If he sees everyone marrying and reproducing, he will simply try to do the same.

For a thinking man, the main thing is to understand who he is within. It is to develop that person within. Doing this creates invisible changes in a man's character. This leads to changing the man's values and behavior. Ultimately this influences achievements. All of these things come through self-awareness and self-education.

Every man was created a one-and-only individual, as a person with a specific gift. The key to your success on planet Earth is to find the field where your gift would be of the highest benefit. Your gift is not what you do but what you are; it is what you were created to be. Your wealth is in your talent and that is why you will be poor until you find yourself. Your gift will make a place for you in the world. When you discover your gift and develop it, the world will start looking for you.

USE NEGATIVE SITUATIONS
TO GAIN EXPERIENCE

Robert Kiyosaki tells a good story of discovering one's gift. When Robert was 9, he spent time with Mike, the father of his friend. He soon began taking financial lessons from Mike. He recounts that he continued to learn from him for the next 30 years. It is the man whom Robert would later refer to as "the rich dad." This "dad" generously gave Robert useful advice on matters regarding money.

Later, Kiyosaki founded his own company that sold nylon wallets. This product was successful in the beginning of Robert's business career. In the early days, it brought him needed income. However, Kiyosaki made various mistakes from time to time, common mistakes that any business person might make. The business began to fail.

He took advantage of a seemingly negative situation. This is a lesson of life and success. No matter what situations you experience in life, think about them as you draw conclusions about what the situations mean for you. Do not allow yourself to obsess on failures. You can choose to have a positive attitude. Look at everything as an opportunity to gain experience.

Robert lost his money by speculating on the stock exchange and an occasional bad investment. His success further declined. However, he did not give up thinking of himself as a successful and prosperous man. His failure motivated him to look at his life goals from a different angle.

He remembered how useful the lessons of the "rich dad", the father of his friend, were in his childhood. He understood how many people were deprived of the chance to be taught about financial principles. Robert found that when he performed a self-assessment: he had a gift to teach people business.

He used his gift to set a goal of teaching others financial principles. The practical experience he had gained by lessons of the "rich dad" and having his own business helped him to take the steps needed to reach his goal. He made correct conclusions from the negative situations that he had experienced and spring boarded into opening a school for training business people about financial principles.

Some things will go wrong for each of us. The most important thing is your attitude in that circumstance. The negative situation that developed, pushed Robert Kiyosaki to fulfill his destination.

You should also pay attention to what happens to you and make sure you draw correct conclusions. Think about your circumstances. What if your failure contains a key to your success and your destination? What if going through hardships gives you precious experience which can help other people, too? If one person managed to turn lemons into lemonade, you can also do it. Just go through your life with your eyes wide open and do not react to failures with a burst of negative emotions. Instead, see the opportunities brought along with every problem you face.

Robert worked hard and gradually won his place in the sun. In 1985, Robert was known as "the tutor of millionaires", in cooperation with Sharon Lecter, created an educational company called "Rich Dad's Organization." The main goal of the company is to teach young people the principles of financial success.

Today, Robert is a successful business advisor. He teaches people how to find financial independence. He never stops passing on this key principle: first you need to believe in your success. Only then will the world believe you.

The experience that Robert gained after his failure now helps other people to rid themselves of financial ignorance. Robert Kiyosaki is the author of over 15 popular books which have sold over 26 million copies. All these books by Kiyosaki are motivational. They stir up the readers' desire to act and improve their lives.

In addition to the lessons of the "rich dad" and the collapse of his own business, the war in Vietnam was also a school of courage and tenacity for him. All of these trials helped Robert to develop the qualities of a successful man. These are tenacity, perseverance, courage and the will to win.

What qualities have you developed? How do you go through your failures? Draw correct conclusions. By properly going through hardships you can develop the qualities of the successful man that is in you. Having gained experience, you can help others and discover your destination and your unique gift.

Robert agrees that the world outside of the front door looks frightening. There, it is difficult to find a job, earn money and find opportunities. However, I can assure you that the life outside the front door is bright and full of life. It is full of optimism and energy. There are countless opportunities. Your life goal and mission is to find your gift, become what you have been created to be and with your gift serve mankind, promoting advancement and influencing humanity in a positive way as Bill Gates, Steve Jobs, Abraham Lincoln and Jesus Christ did.

BECOME WHAT YOU HAVE THE POTENTIAL TO BECOME

Discovering life in oneself is to become what you have the potential to become. It is to become all you can be. It is there in every man but only a few manage to implement it. One of the most important things you need to do is to fulfill your full potential. The efforts you direct at finding and developing the person you are is a key to life.

In order to answer the question "Who am I?" you need to make the following conclusions:

1. You are not your outer appearance, and you are not your body. Your identity should not be fully defined by what you do, by being a manager, a wife, a mother of children or a computer programmer.

2. You should look inside of yourself and see the person who is there. You need to understand what there is inside you. That is where your wealth, your treasure is and comes from, what is inside of you. Recognize yourself as a person who has received a precious gift from your Creator. This gift may be hidden; it may not have been discovered yet and may not have been developed properly. There may be many factors that have distorted the person inside from what you were created to be, but these can be corrected! Read that last sentence again!

3. You can change yourself. Replace the negative traits of your character by the traits you want to have. Working on yourself will reveal a new image of yourself.

4. You hold within you a system of values and beliefs. Forming these comes by determining what they should be and then building them inside of you. In order to build a system of values you need time and persistence.

5. You need to understand what goal you were created for and you need to understand your destination. You need to know your destiny.

THE GOLDEN NUGGETS

1. Who am I? The first question is the most difficult and the most important. You will be someone else until you answer it. Most people play someone else's roles or wear masks of other people because they do not think about what they are created to be.

2. The sooner you answer this important question, "Who am I?" the more effective and successful life you will have.

3. You are God's unique creation. He created you for His high purpose. Discovering and understanding that purpose is important.

4. We are not meant to be a biomass. You were not born to plant a tree, to simply marry, reproduce and die. "I am a human being and I am born with a mission."

5. You need to understand, comprehend and believe, "There is a goal in my birth. I have a mission, and there is something that no one but I can do."

6. You need to maximize your God-given potential through the power of your spirit, your inner core, your values and principles on which your life is based. Your choice of values and determining their priority precedes your goal setting. It is important to build an inner core, form beliefs and life values.

7. The visible success you achieve is the result of what you have done inside you. "*The most important thing is invisible.*" Antoine de Saint-Exupery.

SELF-EXAMINATION TEST

1. **What do you pay more attention to — your appearance or the development of your soul?**
   a) I am trying to look well and wear good clothes to make a good impression (0)
   b) I am trying to comply with fashion and standards of the society but I do not forget about my soul, too (1)
   c) I dedicate major part of my time to self-education and self-development (2)

2. **Do you have your own system of values and beliefs?**
   a) I have no time for that (0)
   b) I did this task at a training session for personal growth (1)
   c) Yes, I have a system of values and beliefs (2)

3. **Can you say that you have built an inner core in you?**
   a) I haven't thought about it yet (0)
   b) I am interested in the topic of personal growth but I did not build my inner core purposefully (1)
   c) Yes, I am working purposefully to form my inner core (2)

4. **Did you happen to miss your bus stop because you were thinking, or do you get distracted during a meeting and miss the question you have been asked?**
   a) Yes, it often happens to me (0)
   b) It happens to me but I work on living a conscious life (1)
   c) I am always here and now (2)

5. **Can you express your opinion in public and defend it even if nobody else supports you?**
   a) No, I seldom speak my opinion in public (0)

b) It is difficult for me to express my opinion aloud but I'm learning to do it (1)

c) I express my opinion openly and I can defend it even if everyone is against me (2)

6. **Do you analyze your behavior; do you ask yourself questions like "Why do I react that way?"**

a) I am very busy and I have no time for such things (0)

b) Sometimes I analyze my behavior and ask such questions (1)

c) I analyze my behavior (2)

7. **Are you engaged in self-education?**

a) I have already received my education (0)

b) I read books in my free time (1)

c) I am engaged in self-education all the time (2)

TEST RESULTS

0–4 points — You haven't taken the time or put forth the effort to ask yourself the question "Who am I?" and do not know the answer yet. You need to work on being in AN active state of consciousness all the time, on being here and now. Create your system of values and beliefs. Work to develop your will power, persistence and tenacity in achieving your goal.

5–9 points — You have already thought over the most vital question, "Who am I?" but you still don't know the answer. Partially you are in the state of active consciousness and you even have your system of values. You need to work more on your self-education and to build purposefully your core, and then the success and actualization of your destination will be guaranteed.

9–12 points — We are happy for you! You know who you are and you have answered the important question. You are always in an active state of mind; you have built your system of values and beliefs, understood your restricting beliefs and worked on them. You have an inner core and you are a mature personality. You are capable of implementing your life missions and fulfilling your destination.

PRACTICAL TASKS

1. **To answer the question "Who am I?"** you will find help in knowledge about the social role, functions, traits of character, genealogical tree and soon.

2. **Find the meaning of your name and surname in an encyclopedia.**

3. **Analyze the following: "What is my family, what amazing things are there about it, what distinctive features it has, what family I come from and what opportunities it brings for me?"**

4. **Try making up a genealogical tree with photographs, names, professions or traits of character which were prominent in your relatives.**

5. **You may want to just describe the social roles and functions that you perform.** For example, mother of father, pastor, businessman, politician, shop assistant and soon it may help your self-identification. Record everything that occurs to you! Your goal is to give a most detailed answer to the question "Who am I?" Remember, the more effort you take, the more you will learn about yourself, and moreover it will result in better progress towards the fulfillment of your destiny and your destination.

Recommended reading

IIIIIIIIIIIIIIIIIIIIIIIIIIIIIIIIIIIIIIIIIIIIIIIIIIIIIIIIIIIIIIIIIIIIIIIIIIIIIIII

For a more detailed study of this topic I recommend reading the books "I am a person. Am I a personality?" and "The art of being here and now" by "The University of Life."

CHAPTER 3

WHAT CAN I DO? A QUESTION OF POTENTIAL

WHAT CAN I DO?
A QUESTION OF
POTENTIAL

Human potential is the ability of a person (individual) or humanity (a group of individuals) to put their theoretical abilities into practice.

The word "potential" comes from the Latin word "*potentia*" which means "strength". Today, potential is defined as a hidden opportunity, ability, strength, that can be displayed under certain circumstances. It is in fact the ability and possibility one has to do or become something.

This means that there is a mighty force, energy, ability inside of us that has not yet been noticed by the world. There are gifts and talents that have not yet been used and power which has not yet been applied. This indicates that we have something very valuable, for which we have not yet found an application in this life. All that you have already done, achieved and opened it is not a potential. But those gifts and talents, which are incorporated in you and have not yet been implemented, make up your potential.

There are different gifts and talents in each of us. Your destination, your special gift, your personal qualities and your potential are interrelated. A great Greek philosopher said you cannot really "know yourself" without knowing your destination. After all, in order to be able to fulfill your mission, you need to understand the unique gift incorporated within you.

You are a special and unique person, who has never lived before and who will never live in the future.

Look at your uniqueness and figure out what distinguishes you from the billions of people who inhabit this planet. Find out for yourself your unique features. Become yourself.

You will only succeed in the field where your gift is. You will only have influence and power in the field of your gifts and talents. The key to your success in this world is to discover the field of your gifts. Your gift is not what you do but who you really are.

What will support you consists in your gift, so until you find yourself you will be poor. The Holy Scriptures teach us that a man's gift opens the way and brings him before great men, all around the world. Neither education, nor good name, nor the color of one's skin or race, nor job, nor career or origin, but a man's gift will give him a freeway in the world. When you discover your gift the whole world will seek you.

Each of us has the ability:

- To create
- To invent
- To dream
- To build

A child is born with a weight of 3kg and eventually grows up to 90kg or even 100kg.

This is a hidden energy in a child that works in all areas of growth and development (growth of muscles, bones etc.). All of these make up a hidden or latent energy.

EVERYTHING HAS LATENT ENERGY

This can be seen even in our hair as it grows again, being cut a week or a month ago. Thus, there is a latent energy in each of us, in all areas of our lives.

WE CAN FIND A LATENT ENERGY INSIDE US

Each of us has a latent energy and we need to discover this invisible "treasure" by way of:

- concentration;
- goal-oriented self-development.

We can achieve even more than we could expect if we try to be less distracted by the fuss of life and concentrate more on developing some qualities or characteristic of our soul and our character. All great and successful people did so: they stayed alone with themselves to develop their gift.

Even if you are a loser today, it does not mean that you cannot change yourself.

You already have the most important tool — work.

So if you work on yourself:

- intellectually;
- spiritually;
- physically

you will be able to realize your potential.

Stephen King has sold 350 million copies of his books. How? He became a slave of his gift, his talent. This is wonderful! He is not a slave of circumstances or people. He writes 10 pages of text every day without a lunch break, regardless of public holidays and weekends. Thomas Edison worked 18 hours a day and the result of his submission to his gift are 1093 U.S patents registered in his name, as well as many patents in the United Kingdom, France and Germany.

It is not easy — it is hard work. Edison was able to go through the pain and suffering, devoting himself to his gift. As a result, he managed to become the person that we know him to be — a great genius of an inventor.

Each of these great people understood who they were, found out the unique features of their personalities, discovered their special gifts, their purpose and served with their gift, bringing progress to the world.

Anyone who wants to be a great and influential person should be ready to pay the highest price in order to develop their gift and to submit themselves to this gift.

What does it mean to submit oneself to one's gift? This means to submit oneself to education and self-development and to devote enough time to improve one's gift.

Actually, you may be more talented than Leonardo da Vinci, Leo Tolstoy, Oprah Winfrey or Steve Jobs. I mean potentially, of course. But the world will never know about you because you have not become a slave of your gift. You did not spend sleepless nights over manuscripts, you were not exhausted, you did not work hard enough you did not drain all your potential to the last drop. You were not bold, you did not take a risk, and you did not cross the limits of yourself. You did not stay alone for days on end in your laboratory as Thomas Edison did, having forgotten about everything else in order to focus and create a new product.

Michael Jordan is an outstanding athlete and basketball player, who has shown very good results during ten years and set several world records that other athletes have not been able to improve yet. He developed his gift, and that is why he is well-known all over the world.

Michael Jordan speaks about himself: "At school when I was a little boy, I was told: "You will never play basketball. You're too skinny, you have no coordination, and you cannot think properly, you cannot find your way in the field". But I was obsessed with basketball. Every morning I woke up at 5am, went to the gym, where I would throw the ball for 3 hours before school. There were cockroaches and rats everywhere in the darkness, but every day in the morning, with tears in my eyes, I continued to train and improve my movements. Every day for three years in a row, I kept on training. Once, one of the starting players on the team turned his ankle so he could not continue playing. They called me: "Come here, do you know how to play?" "Yes, I do." "Well, come on, go and replace him!" He went to the court and began to throw the ball into the basket. The whole place exploded: "Wow! and again and again!" The coach says, "Stay on the court, WE WILL FIND A PLACE FOR YOU ON THE TEAM!"

Now he is paid $30 million just for allowing a company or brand to use his name, but the secret of his success lies in the fact that he perfected his gift and worked frantically toward his potential. He KNEW who HE WAS, What HIS POTENTIAL WAS and pressed towards it with all that he had within him.

Michael found out who he was. He revealed his gift and was able to make it almost perfect. Now this well-developed person is fulfilling his mission, plays basketball, enjoys the game and pleases others. Many of us will never realize who we are because we do not want to go through the pain and trials. We do NOT believe in ourselves.

Which of us will consciously decide to suffer pain, discomfort and inconvenience? It is much easier to sit in front of your

TV watching people like Michael Jordan. You feel better now, but it is temporary because at the end of your life you will regret it: every man has a need to be great at something.

In fact, the truth of life is that almost all that we achieve through pain is the best medicine for us, as most drugs are bitter. We do not like to eat lettuce because we're not animals to eat leaves. It tastes much better to eat a cake or a candy. Yet in fact, these products are the most hazardous to our health. Lettuce is not particularly tasty, but very useful. It is bitter but useful. Similarly, most of what is now "bitter" for our old nature is going to be useful for our future.

Working to perfect our gift and overcoming the pain of self-discipline, we achieve our goals and move on to our dreams. Each of us needs to find our own special gift and perfect it; we need to focus on our gift and never allow ourselves to be distracted from the execution of our purpose.

You should not think on a small scale. You are a gift to the entire planet Earth. Do not die without realizing yourself; inside you there is something that the whole world needs.

Neurologist Daniel Levitin writes: *"After numerous studies we came to see the following rule: whatever field one chooses to achieve, the level of skill commensurate with the status of a world-class expert, it requires 10,000 hours of practice. No matter whom you take — composers, basketball players, writers, skaters, pianists, chess players and inveterate criminals and soon — we meet this figure with a surprising regularity. Ten thousand hours means approximately three hours of practice per day, or twenty hours per week for the past ten years. Yet there is not a single case of a person who achieved the highest level of skill in a less period of time."*

Actor Michael Masterson claimed that there are four levels of having a skill: incompetence, competence, excellence and virtuosity: To overcome incompetence, you must practice about 1,000 hours in your chosen field.

To achieve excellence, you need to continue your training until you reach the total amount of 5,000 hours. Virtuosity is extremely rare. You cannot reach it by just practicing. You will also need a natural talent, but even in this case, the training will take you at least 10,000 hours. (Malcolm Gladwell. *"Geniuses and outsiders: why some get everything and the others get nothing?"*)

Thus, the magic number leading to make your gift perfect is 10,000 hours of preparation.

American scientists say that people get more success in the area that they consider their hobby. Hobby is a kind of human activity, a kind of occupation that a person pursuits in his free time. The main purpose of a hobby is to promote one's self-actualization. Hobbies may eventually grow into a major activity that brings money. "That would be perfect if you engage in an activity which you like, and besides, it brings you money," that is, a hobby may eventually grow into a job. Do one thing, but do it well. It is easy.

FOCUS ON ONE THING, AND DO NOT SCATTER YOUR ATTENTION

Purposefulness is a must. Gather all your efforts to achieve a single goal — and you will be bound to succeed.

Success will bring recognition, money, and all other pleasures of life. For the present time, just do your job well!

"Whatever you do, be the best in your business" — advises Genichi Kawakami, the President of Yamaha Motor Company;

its motorcycles, creativity and a spirit of competition and a fearsome leader in the world racing competitions.

Once upon a time Robin Sharma was a highly paid, overworked lawyer who specialized in civil claims. He was tired of living such a life without sense and purpose. Emptiness and lack of motivation made him look for answers and inspiration in the works of Og Mandino, Norman Vincent Peale, Gandhi, Albert Einstein, Nelson Mandela and others.

A few months after he started to put their lessons into practice, Sharma felt that his thoughts, his tone, his whole life had drastically changed for the better. Sharma gave up a well-paid legal practice and became a writer and a professional speaker.

Today he lives a life that can only be envied. He earns his living by traveling around the world and giving inspirational lectures on motivation in different places: in Hawaii, Israel and Europe. He has a wonderful purpose in life — freedom; and he earns more money than before when he was a highly paid lawyer. He loves his job and he is happy.

After he discovered himself and his uniqueness, Robin found his destiny. He dared to ask "who am I?" and he dared to make major changes to reach his newly discovered destiny.

"Being rich and having a lot of money is not the same thing. A truly rich person is the one who is satisfied with his life." (THE GREEK PHILOSOPHER DIOGENES)

It is the perfect scenario, when you are living your dream, when you have found your gift and you are working to bring it to perfection. The worse scenario is when you do not know the purpose of your day to day existence. And you feel that you are just a small component in a big machine that has no real meaning.

When Adam disobeyed God, he lost his greatness; he lost contact with his field or gift: that is why he had to work so hard. You work hard and sweat it out only when doing something for which you were not born.

Buckminster Fuller once stood on the shore of Lake Michigan and seriously contemplated suicide. He thought himself a failure, a "salvaged" man. Even worse, he had no motivation to find a new job and continue to work within that corrupt system which threw him into the street through no fault of his. The work did not bring him any satisfaction, but also it was a reason of constant stress and could not give him enough money for living. "The choice was to jump or to think," he remembered. He chose to think.

Life without knowing your destiny leads to "rat races" (an endless, self- defeating and pointless pursuit which is associated with futile efforts of a laboratory rat trying to escape from a labyrinth), depression and frustration, and attempts to commit suicide. At the last moment, he decided to arrange "an experiment to see what can one man do for the good of the world and all mankind" instead of just killing himself.

Fuller decided to do something that he liked; to devote himself to his favorite occupation.

Supported by a group of professors and students at a small college in North Carolina, he started to work on a project that later brought him fame and revolutionized the engineering — the geodesic dome.

He had shown courage to leave the work which had not given him any satisfaction and believed that his gift, his invention, will support his life although he was ready to work on his invention even for free. He had to develop his gift, to ensure that his invention would be put into practice. In a few years, there were thousands of such domes all over the world. Later on, Fuller has not stopped in the development of his gift, his potential.

All his life (he died at age 88), he brought his gifts to the world, not only as an inventor but also as a writer, educator, philosopher and poet. His inventions and discoveries still help the advance of science; they make our lives better and more comfortable. His goal was to make the life of every person on earth better, to help people discover and realize their potential.

As soon as Fuller had decided to discover himself, open up his gift and realize his potential, his life changed.

Dear reader! Each of us is capable of doing the same: the choice is ours. Everyone can find the field in which he is gifted, his favorite activity and devote his time to it, instead of working for a good income, but no satisfaction. Ask yourself: what is my favorite occupation? If you can devote yourself to it without getting money for your work, but in order to discover your potential, then you will find out who you are, release the invisible potential and begin to do things you were born for. A bird is flying without taking great efforts to cut the air with its wings; it is just brought along by the air. It is born to do this without much training. When you find out the field where you are gifted, what you were created for, you will not have to work hard and sweat it out. You will get guaranteed success.

"When I was 17, I read a quote that went some-thing like: "If you live each day as if it was your last, some day you will certainly be right." It impressed me, and since then, for the last 33 years, I looked in the mirror every morning and asked myself: "If today was the last day of my life, would I want to do what I am about to do today? And whenever the answer has been "No" for several days in a row, I know I need to change something." (STEVE JOBS)

Rich people do not work for money, they are doing what they like to do, devote themselves to the work they love and do not wait for a well-deserved rest or retirement, but keep on working passionately until the end of their lives.

"I do not want to retire. I love my job. I've always said that if people stop attending my concerts, I will continue to do the same, but as a hobby. I see myself at the age of ninety, as I am rolled out onto the stage in a wheelchair, and I play "Yesterday" very slowly. However, things are different now, just the contrary. We enjoy playing music, the audience enjoys our music, and we all do it, we will con-tinue living in the same way." (PAUL MCCARTNEY)

"Sometimes life hits you over the head with a brick. Do not lose faith. I am convinced: the only thing that gave me the strength to go on was love of my work. Find your love. This advice applies not only to relations with the people, but also to work. Work occupies the largest part of your life, and the only way to achieve true satisfaction is to work so that you can be proud of the results." (STEVE JOBS)

When creating Facebook, Mark Zuckerberg was not thinking about profit or money that this business could bring him. He was just doing things he truly loved. In this activity, the creator of the well-known social network sees the reason for his success. According to him, he was not even going to create a company, but simply did something he wanted to see in the world today. But in order for it to be a comfortable social network, you need a lot of users. *"For me, Facebook is neither work nor pleasure. This is my mission, something that gives me energy, and it is the only thing I can do in this life,"* believes Mark Zuckerberg. By the age of 29, the creator of the largest social network and the idol of millions is one of the youngest billionaires in the world (his wealth is estimated by Forbes to be about $13.3 billion). As you can see, this man met his opportunity when he did things he loved — things that inspired him.

Mark discovered himself and found his destiny, his life mission; he does what he likes, he is happy, and he earns millions.

So, each of us has a special gift and it takes time to discover it. When you discover the gift in yourself, you need to submit yourself to the gift and improve it, as all well-known and famous people did. You should do it if you do not want to live the life of an ordinary person. When you dedicate yourself to your gift and do all the necessary studies to fully explore your field, you will be able to serve and to live a full-valued and meaningful life.

CONCLUSIONS

1. You need to find your gift, something that differs you from others, something you are doing better than others, something you can achieve better than others, something you love doing.

2. One of the main keys to discovering your gift is the question, "What is my favorite occupation?" If you can dedicate yourself to it, not for money, but simply to reveal your potential — by doing this you will discover your potential and start to fulfill your mission.

3. In the future, each of us must have enough courage to follow our gift or to be engaged in a favorite occupation, even if it does not bring you any income at the moment. Many well-known and successful people have taken a risk and won — remember the stories of Robin Sharma and Buckminster Fuller.

4. Next, we need to apply the rule of 10,000 hours, because, in order to achieve the level of a skill commensurate with the status of a world-class expert, we need to practice for 10,000 hours. Remember, each of us needs to be the best in our field.

THE GOLDEN NUGGETS

1. Potency is defined as a hidden opportunity, ability, strength, being able to display itself in certain conditions. This means that there is a mighty force, energy and ability inside us that has not yet been noticed by the world.

2. To give life to yourself means to become a person you are potentially and realize your potential. Therefore, the most important result of the efforts of man is the effort of self-development and continuous growth.

3. You will be successful only in the field of your gift. You will be influential and powerful in the field of your gift and talent. The key to your success in the world is to discover the field of your gift.

4. If you work on yourself:

   - intellectually
   - spiritually
   - physically

   you will be able to realize your potential.

5. In order to make your gift perfect, you need to work on yourself but it hurts. Overcoming the pain of self-discipline, we achieve our goals and move towards our dream.

6. If you submit yourself to your gift, you will become known and influential; people will seek you and invite you, you will get well-paid because you have perfected your gift.

7. Anyone who wants to be a great and influential person should be willing to pay the highest price, in order to develop their gift and to submit themselves to this gift.

8. From numerous studies, we came to discover the following rule: whatever field one chooses to achieve the level of skill commensurate with the status of a world class expert, it requires 10,000 hours of practice. No matter whom you analyze — composers, basketball players, writers, skaters, pianists, chess players, and inveterate criminals and so on — this figure appears with a surprising regularity. Ten thousand hours is approximately three hours of practice per day, or twenty hours per week for the period of ten years.

9. Rich people do not work for money, they are doing what they like to do; they devote themselves to a job they love and do not live waiting for a well-deserved rest or retirement, but work passionately until the end of their lives.

SELF-EXAMINATION TEST

1. **Do you know your unique gift?**
   a) I do not think I have any unique gifts (0)
   b) I am engaged in the search of my gifts and talents (1)
   c) Yes, I know my unique gift (2)

2. **Did you happen to be so passionately excited about your favorite occupation (computer games excluded) that you forgot about the time and meals?**
   a) I never forget about meals (0)
   b) One or two times in my life (1)
   c) Yes, it happens to me often when I am doing things I love (2)

3. **Are you ready to apply the rule of 10,000 hours to become an expert with your gift?**
   a) Absolutely not. I'm too busy at work (0)
   b) I am developing my gift, but give it less time (1)
   c) I am ready to spend time to perfect my gift (2)

4. **Can you work alone for a long time, without communicating with friends and entertainment?**
   a) It is difficult for me to be alone (0)
   a) I can work alone, if I am carried away by the activity (1)
   b) I love to be alone, especially when I am busy with the things I love (2)

5. **Are you ready to devote yourself to the development of your unique gift, to be a servant of your gift?**
   a) To do it, I will have to quit my job (0)
   b) I am trying to develop my talent, but not so fanatically (1)
   c) I am completely dedicated to my gift already (2)

Test Results

0–4 points — We are sorry to say that but you do not work to realize your potential. You need to make a decision to realize yourself. In order to do it you have to conquer your laziness and, under the rule of 10,000 hours, to devote every day of your life to improving yourself and your gift.

5–9 points — You are partially trying to realize your potential, but you need a serious commitment. Show perseverance and persistence, devote your time to work, apply the rule of 10,000 hours, and you will realize your potential.

9–12 points — We are happy for you! You are dedicated to realize your potential. Every day you devote time to developing your gift. You will become a real expert in your field and the world will know your name soon!

PRACTICAL TASKS

1. **Write down your wildest dreams about your achievements; remember the boldest predictions of other people about you.**

2. **What kind of problems are you meant to solve?** What makes you worry most of all? What do you dislike? What are you ready to spend your efforts on to change it?

Recommended reading

||||||||||||||||||||||||||||||||||||||||||||||||||||||||||||||||||||||||||

For a more detailed study of this topic I recommend you to read the book "Where you can get money for your dream" by "The University of Life."

CHAPTER 4

WHY AM I HERE? WHAT AM I DOING HERE?

WHY AM I HERE? WHAT AM I DOING HERE?

God made a human being from clay and there was one un-used piece left.

- What else should I make for you? — God asked.
- Shape happiness — the human being begged. God said nothing and put the remaining piece of clay into the human's hand.

The main point of this parable is the following: "Only you are responsible for your life and for making it a happy life". The happy life is impossible without finding an answer to the question "Why am I here? What am I doing here?"

It is the question of the purpose of your living and your life destination. I was born with a mission. I was born with a definite purpose on planet Earth, and here I should complete my goal and fulfill my destination.

Each of us should realize the importance of having a talk with our own soul: "I am not just a piece of meat which was born like an animal: I was not born with a purpose of planting a tree. I was not born with a purpose of marrying and giving life to a son — animals are able to have children too and they can have many more children than we do. My mission does not consist in my appearance, a beautiful haircut or in showing off my body, decorations, and clothes. I do not have a mission to study at a popular institution of higher education, to build a country-house and be proud of its building.

The most essential thing is the following: my mission is to identify the purpose of my coming on this planet and, having identified it, to complete and achieve it. Certainly, a lot of time should be spent on finding it, determining my destination, but life being full of sense and devotion to a significant goal, makes looking for my destination a significant goal."

Do not underestimate yourself! Do not depreciate a creation of God. It is important to create a family and bring up children: these things are good and even necessary. However, your discovery and realization of your personality for the well-being of humanity is much more essential. Identifying the purpose of your living is more important than creating a family and having children. If you are not aware of the goal of your living, what you will do when your children grow up and leave your house? Are you going to grasp at them as if they were a straw to save you? So many mothers are unable to let their children go into the adult life and become literally attached to them giving rise to co-dependency. In this case, children cannot make up their mind to leave parent's home and start to live independently; therefore, they become a type of an eternal teenager hanging on to their mother's apron strings.

It is inevitable that being unaware of the purpose for your life, you will not be able to recover from being abandoned by your wife or husband. Even a good family can become a trap for one's destiny when the family becomes your aim. Some people live for the sake of their partners and derive their strength and energy from them. When the relationship is over, the strength for life is gone and there is no more energy to live. The source of life's energy comes from our Creator and Maker. We did not decide to be born; hence we cannot live on our own.

When you know your mission and life goal, you will be better able to avoid these life traps.

Kate was a quiet and calm child; she did not create any problems for her parents. Her mother directed her life easily. Early on, she chose her surroundings and her friends, and then she helped her choose the school she would attend after high school. After she graduated from the university, Kate listened to her mother's advice and chose a job of her mother's choosing. Later, when her family decided to change their citizenship and left for another country, Kate went with them. She was fond of the new country; she rented an apartment with her friends and kept on studying and working. However, her mother disliked the new country. Soon she resolved that they needed to come back because she had difficulties adapting to life in a new place. Despite her daughter's desire to stay in this new country, her mother insisted that she return to the old country with them. (Otherwise, her meaning of life consisting in interfering into Kate's affairs would be lost.) Kate had to follow her parents and come back to her homeland where she did not have such a wide range of opportunities as before. Having come back, Kate remained dependent on her mother. Her mother continued directing Kate's life. She wanted to have grandchildren. So, she ordered her daughter to have them in spite of her being not married. The reason was very important: Kate should bear a child while her parents are still capable of helping her to bring the baby up. Soon twins were born. Now Kate and her mom are busy bringing up the twins.

Let's sum up this story. Kate's mother does not know the aim of her own existence. She devoted her life to her daughter and Kate is the meaning of it. She did not let her go and controlled her life because of this co-dependence. To have a break in their relationship meant she was to lose the meaning of her life.

She did not let Kate build her life independently without her influence. A lot of mother's act in a similar way because they incorrectly see the meaning of their lives as being the designer or creator of their child's life. If such mothers answered the question "What things should I do here, on this planet Earth?" they would start thinking about their destination. Then, they would let their children go into adult life and would be busy implementing their own goals.

Kate never managed to get detached from her mother and kept on living in concordance with her decisions. Indeed, from the Creator's point of view, it is a miserable sight. The girl is ignorant of whom she is destined to be, she did not find her destination and her gift. As a result, Kate and her mother bring up twins all day and night and have poor financial stability. Kate does not have any time to look for an answer to the question "Why am I here?", she does not know that it is the most essential aspect in her life, therefore she will not be able to teach it to her children and, perhaps, the situation with Kate and her mother will repeat again — this time, with Kate and her children. God gives an adult the freedom of choice! It is rather a grievous story.

Dear women, do not marry until you find your true being, your mission. Do not be afraid of living without family — be afraid of living an empty and meaningless life.

What does it mean — to know one's life mission?

The mission is to:

1. Find your gift, the thing you were created for, the thing that inspires you and the thing you are fond of doing, and the thing you are doing better than others.

2. Realize that your gift does not only belong to you. Your calling is to serve people and humanity with this gift.

You can be a millionaire and your firm can make a contribution to the development of humanity just as Apple once did it. Having become rich, you can donate your money to charity. You can become a politician and improve the institutions of power in your country. You can become a model of a perfect man or a devoted husband and a father in order to show the role of a man's responsibility for the family, earth and the generations to come. Only you are responsible for the development of your gift and for its brilliance after the process of its refinement.

Everything is meant for something in this life. The snakes that so many fears were meant to fulfill their life destination as well as mosquitoes, birds and trees. Our ignorance of the meaning of the existence of one or another creation does not mean they are meaningless. Our reaction such as fear or disgust does not cancel the meaning of their existence because every creation serves a definite purpose. Likewise, a lack of knowledge about your life mission does not abolish the mission itself.

Consequently, every creation exists with a definite purpose and takes part in one big plan no matter how insignificant it can seem to be. There are no organs inside your body that do not serve a vital purpose.

The same happens in nature. People noticed that every plant and animal is meant to maintain the natural balance. Any disturbance of this balance has an impact on everything.

You can be used by someone for their aims when you are not aware of your true being. Ignorance of one's life mission leads to one's life being used improperly. If you are not aware of your destination, you are likely to become used by someone in accordance with his purposes and to work for a person who knows his plans and goals. You can be a small element in a corporate system serving your boss all your life and you will retire unsatisfied with your way of living.

Once I saw a refrigerator at a friend's apartment. Having opened it I was surprised to see it used for a different purpose than cooling food — it was full of canned food and grits. As it appeared, the fridge was broken and they used it as a cupboard. It occurred to me that it was a good model of human life. Each of us has our destination and target, but when we ignore it, we are used for purposes other than for what we were actually intended.

Exploitation for other purposes happens only when we are living outside the design of the Creator's intention.

If you do not know how to use an object properly, it is possible that you will use it for something other than the purpose it was intended for. You can be a sincere person devoting yourself to your husband, child or boss, but your sincerity cannot, and will not, fill the gap in your knowledge about your life purpose. You cannot realize why they live next to you and in such a way you endanger yourself and other people as well. Kate's mother set an obstacle in her daughter's way insisting on her bearing a child without first being married. Perhaps, she also deprived her of the chance for another life — far away from her homeland. Not only did she fail to teach her the rules of life, but she also did not let her find the purpose of living and she stopped Kate's development by her actions. Kate was never given the chance to answer the question "Why am I here?"

If you want to identify the purpose of a thing, only its Creator can provide you with an answer.

Only the inventor of iPad knows about the purpose of its creation and how to use it.

Only the inventor of a mobile phone or any other device or medicine can know precisely how to use it.

Having bought a laptop, you are not going to use it as a tray. On the contrary, having paid for it from your own pocket you will take care of its safety and read a user's manual before working with it. By way of the manual, the manufacturer of this device explains to you the purpose of its creation and the rules for its proper use.

Most people do not know what they are living for. Asking a question of the purpose of their existence would be an absurd thing to do merely on this account. You will never answer the questions "Why am I here? What am I living for?" while you keep on asking other creatures about who you really are.

You should have a personal link to the Creator! You must ask the Creator a question "What am I living for?". A man cannot be aware of his destination without the help of his Creator.

There is one thing that makes a human being differ from any other beings and proves that the human has a Creator. It is his inner voice known as intuition. Intuition is beyond the scope of our mind. It is surprising, but it is a fact of life. Your inner "I" somehow knows the purpose of your existence. Lend an ear to your inner voice and intuition. Find some time to seclude yourself from the fuss of life and be face to face with yourself and God.

Accept yourself in the way you were created by God, do not imitate anyone else. He created you with your special features because He was aware of your destination. The iPhone has its own characteristics that are different from the characteristics of any other cell phone on account of their having a different field of application. In the same way, you are created with your special features that you need to fulfill your destiny and why it is so important to accept them.

Talk to the Creator in a state of peace and solitude and ask Him a question concerning the purpose of your living.

Have you ever experienced uneasiness when being alone? Sometimes it even frightens us. After a short-term of isolation, we desperately reach for our cell phones and are dying to engage in our usual affairs or join a group of acquaintances in order to satisfy our emotional passions. Why is it so difficult to be face to face with your own inner world? Perhaps, it is because we are not ready to run into ourselves. We are not aware of our true being, which is why we feel discomfort as if we are among unfamiliar people. Then it is not strange that we do not have any desire to be in God's presence, whom we know even less and even do not see.

But how can we identify our true being as created by God? People can be cunning, imperfect and selfish, so how can we separate ourselves from these impurities?

> *"You do not need to leave your room. Remain sitting at your table and listen. Do not even listen, just wait. Be quiet, still and solitary. The world will freely offer itself to you without its disguise. It has no choice. It will roll in ecstasy at your feet."* (FRANZ KAFKA)

What simplicity and depth this quote has. How practical everything seems to be!

Only in a state of solitude, when you willingly stay face to face with God, can He help you to open yourself, show the impurities preventing you from moving forward and help you to identify your unique gift, life mission and destination.

You should keep calm and listen to the voice inside you. It can be your inner voice, your intuition. You might have a strong desire or a passion for being engaged in a certain activity, but you did not dare to start or did not even think about.

Your destiny provides you with answers to questions concerning you overcoming different obstacles, hassles and giving you a vision of your future. Your goal and destination also fill your life with meaning and make it significant. Purposeless life will definitely be gray, monotonous, ordinary and frustrating.

"Do not work for attaining success, but work for having a meaning of life." (ALBERT EINSTEIN)

Do not look for a man to learn about the purpose of your life, but look for the Creator, who is your Maker. Identify your life mission and gift. Answer the question "What am I living for?" and become a master in this field, serve others with your gift, because you were created exactly with this goal.

"Your time is limited, so don't waste it by living someone else's life. Don't be trapped by dogmas which are only a result of other people's thinking. Don't let the noise of other opinions muffle your own inner voice. The most important thing is to have the courage to follow your heart and intuition. Somehow, they already know what you truly want to become. Everything else is secondary." (STEVE JOBS)

CONCLUSIONS

1. You must find your own gift, the activity you are fond of and the activity you were created for.

2. You must become aware of the need to serve humanity with your gift. Go and venture! You should not give up after failures because this gift does not belong only to you. You were created to serve people with your gift.

3. You must ask your Creator for the purpose of your living because only He knows your destiny. You cannot ask this question to other people; only the Creator knows the intention of His creation.

4. Accept yourself in the way you are created. You are a unique individual with your own special features that you need to carry on your life mission.

5. Find time for a private conversation with your Creator so that you can ask Him about the purpose of your existence.

6. You should calm down and listen to the voice of your heart. This is your inner voice, your intuition or strong desire or a passion to a certain kind of activity.

THE GOLDEN NUGGETS

1. I was born with a mission and definite purpose and I must achieve my goal and fulfill my destiny on the planet Earth.

2. To have a mission is to:

   - Find your own gift: a thing you were created for, a thing that inspires you the most, a thing you are fond of doing, a thing that you can do better than others.
   - Realize that your gift does not belong merely to you. You are called to serve people and humanity with your talent.

3. Every human being needs to find the meaning of life and receive a satisfaction in it.

4. Everyone has his own purpose of existence.

5. Destination is a primordial intention born in the mind of the Creator that prompted him to create a certain object of inanimate nature, animate nature and the highest creature, a human being.

6. Only your Maker is aware of the purpose of your creation.

SELF-EXAMINATION TEST

1. **Do you consider planting a tree, building a house and bearing a son to be the purpose of your life?**
   a) Yes, I have such a goal (0)
   b) It is very essential but I am looking for the meaning of my life too (1)
   c) I am aware of my destiny and do my best to fulfill it (2)

2. **Is creation of a family and bearing a child the main purpose of your life?**
   a) Yes, it is extremely important (0)
   b) I think of self-realization as a personality beyond family (1)
   c) I live with a purpose of fulfilling my destiny (2)

3. **The main goal of a man is to carry on his life's destiny. What attitude do you have towards this statement?**
   a) I believe that creation of family and giving birth to my heirs are the most essential things to do (0)
   b) Family is important, but I am also engaged in identifying my destination (1)
   c) I completely agree with this point of view (2)

4. **Do you know your gift and talent?**
   a) I do not have any gifts or talents (0)
   b) I am looking for my gift (1)
   c) I am aware of my gift and work to achieve progress in self-development in this field (2)

TEST RESULTS

0–4 scores — We regret it but you do not know your destiny and think that living for visible things is the most necessary. You are not apt to waste your time on philosophy. We advise you to reflect on the purpose of your coming to this planet, because meaningless life breeds internal emptiness, depression and mental disorders.

5–9 scores — You are trying to find yourself, but your attempts were not successful. You will find practical advice to help you to identify your true being in the second part of the book.

9–12 scores — We are happy for you! You have devoted yourself to fulfillment of your destiny. You will have great success and satisfaction in life.

PRACTICAL TASKS

1. **"What am I living for?"** — How do you think; what
    intention did God have when creating you?

2. **What problems do you need to resolve?** What things still
    make you worry? What seems wrong to you? What are you
    ready to spend your efforts on to improve it and alter your life?

3. **Reflect upon your origin (for example, your origin is
    God; He is a source of your opportunities, strengths and
    abilities).** Write down the thoughts that you have during
    reflection and exploration of different books, films etc.

Recommended reading

||||||||||||||||||||||||||||||||||||||||||||||||||||||||||||||||||||||||||||||

*I advise you to read the book "Where you can
get money for your dream" by "The University
of Life" in order to study this topic better.*

CHAPTER 5

WHERE AM I GOING? A QUESTION OF DESTINY

WHERE AM I GOING? A QUESTION OF DESTINY

"Never step away from your goal — this is a tool to extend time and it is a very effective tool but using it is not easy." (GEORGE CHRISTOPHE LICHTENBERG)

Where am I going? This is the question of purpose and destiny. The most important thing is to know the purpose of your calling, your vocation. The global question is why you came to the planet Earth. During seminars, speakers call on us to write down our 10 main goals and set time frames for achieving them. We write everything down, make a decision and very often we never even take the first step to what we just vowed to do.

This is a grave mistake. When we don't come closer to the goal and don't make everyday steps for achieving it, we will not get the results we inwardly set out to attain. We wind up disappointed with our life and end up depressed because we have wasted it. On the other hand, when we achieve our goal we are satisfied and build a good self-esteem.

Where am I going? — This is the question of your birth purpose on the earth. Why did I arrive in this world at this time? Have you ever thought about it? What are you living for?

What is the purpose of you waking up every morning, brushing your teeth, having breakfast and going to work? Is there any sense in your actions? Is there a purpose in your existence?

Unfortunately, our society is a victim of such a world system which does not encourage people to live consciously and become who they were called to be. The system wants to control people and rule them for its own purposes.

People often are only "parts of a system". That is why they got used to living automatically, working from morning till night until they are old, just spending their lives like this. It is easier to control these people as if they are a herd. A person who is not the unique person that God created them to be, who doesn't know his calling and purpose of his life, doesn't reflect on the question "Where am I going?"

When we set up a goal for ourselves our body starts to:

- produce inner energy independently
- mobilize all its strength in one direction

Our body is designed to work for reaching a set goal. The set goal can release inner capacities and involve all human potential.

CONSEQUENCES OF LACKING A GOAL

When there is no specific task, the human's subconscious mind will be in a passive state. That is why, when the goal is badly stated or it does not exist at all, our sub-conscious will automatically conceive it as unreachable, as impossible as to find a solution for something that does not exist.

The human brain consists of two parts — consciousness and subconsciousness.

1. Consciousness is responsible for the decision-making process.

2. Subconsciousness is searching for the ways of their implementation and fulfillment.

Consciousness creates a request for an information search in our brain, in our "hard disk" — in our sub-consciousness. One part of the brain "says" which task is necessary to be accomplished, the other one "thinks" about how to do that. The first one is will and the second one is vast resources.

Consciousness sets goals independently, achieves them through will and evaluation of results. Sub-consciousness doesn't set its own goals but helps to achieve the goals that have already been set.

Unfortunately, people don't know how they are created and live making grave mistakes, losing their peace, destroying their mentality and failing to fulfill their callings.

Most young ladies don't understand that first and primary they need to find and fulfill their life calling, i.e. to become the person God created them to be. To bear a child or to get married is not the primary goal for a lady who wants to become successful in life. Actually the role of a fiancée, wife or mother has nothing to do with it. But ladies are living in a world of illusion which makes them merely "breeding pigs" and are thoughtlessly longing "for something I don't know what." A foreign man left his contact details on a dating website. In his questionnaire, he wrote that he wanted to get acquainted with a woman aged 25 to 35. In a few days, he was almost ready to take the website owner to court. What happened is that his request attracted many letters from ladies and women living in countries that were struggling with reconstruction after wars and economic struggles. In their letters, they sent their provocative photos in swimsuits, and their age was also different from what he asked for — from 17 to 50.

The foreigner was shocked. He thought that such a big number of letters was a joke, and that is why he wanted to take the website owner to Court. He couldn't even imagine that women would offer themselves in such a shameless and vulgar way as if they were inanimate objects.

This kind of attitude in women is caused by the fact that they didn't answer the question "Where am I going?" and they didn't know their true life purpose and did not realize their value. To them, their life purpose seems to consist of creating a family, and that is why the search for a husband takes first place in their lives. They had heard that all was fair in love and war and therefore, saw all methods as a valid way of fulfilling this purpose.

Look at women who don't have a husband and children, and instead of being happy because they have extra time for:

- Self-development
- Realization of potential and
- Establishing themselves as real persons and personalities

...they cry, immerse themselves into depression and wrongly think that family will make them happy. That could be funny if it wasn't so sad!

Actually, before creating a family, it is necessary for a person to be already happy; otherwise, she will destroy her partner's life. After a baby is born, the process of creating herself and self-realization are becoming less important, the woman doesn't really have time to release her potential and develop her personality.

Most people live under the influence of the wrong and common belief which says that the sense of man's life is to grow a tree, build a house and bring up a son. But nobody is paying attention to the fact that first of all, a man has to build himself and become a personality. As a result, we have divorces and broken families because families are created by unprepared people, in some sense, even by underdeveloped people, who are mentally equal to teenagers, though adult by their age; they are immature in a moral aspect.

All great and famous people understand that the chief priority in their life is to discover oneself, one's calling and to devote one's life to its fulfillment; all the other things will come later.

Think about the following quotation. It might help you:

"We're here to make a contribution to the world. Otherwise, why should we be here? Did you know that you have good things to accomplish in life? And did you know that those good things are getting rather dusty while you pour yourself another cup of coffee, and decide not to think about them instead of bringing them into your life? We were all born with a gift to bring into life. This gift is, in fact, our purpose, our calling. And you don't need permission to decide on your own purpose. No boss, teacher, parent, priest or other authority can decide it for you. Just find that unique purpose." (STEVE JOBS)

People who simply live their life and care only about bearing children are under the influence of a misbelief that they are people.

The life of such people is similar to the life of animals that leave many offspring. Our children and grand-children will not make us people; their availability does not make us different from animals. A person who doesn't do anything for the fulfillment of his goal and mission on earth is a "living dead" because he didn't create the unique individual inside himself that he was born to be and his life has no purpose.

> *"Only the goal gives meaning and satisfaction to life. It promotes health and gives you a drop of optimism in hard times."* (STEVE JOBS)

"Some people die at 25 but they aren't buried until they are 75". This was said by Benjamin Franklin, an American scientist and politician.

A person becomes a real individual when he has set and accurately defined his goals. In order to fulfill their plans, many well-known politicians spend a huge and vast amount of emotional and intellectual resources. They make big efforts to achieve their goals.

Many actors spend 18 hours a day working on their roles in order to succeed in their field.

> *"Every person is given only one life and everyone deserves a chance for success especially if he is ready to work hard."* (BENAZIR BHUTTO)

The history of Benazir Bhutto's life, who was the Prime Minister of the Islamic Republic of Pakistan and was the first woman elected the head of an Islamic state government. This is an unbelievable but true fact!

Benazir Bhutto was born in Pakistan on 21 June, 1953. Benazir's father was a progressive person who brought up his daughter differently. He parted from the traditional ways of Islamic statutes. The father saw Benazir Bhutto as a parliamentarian.

In April 1969, Bhutto went to Radcliffe College at Harvard University in the United States. There she "felt the taste of democracy for the first time." In 1973, she graduated from Harvard University and obtained a Bachelor's Degree *cum laude* in public administration.

Benazir Bhutto conducted many important reforms in Pakistan and people valued her for it.

In her youth, Benazir gave herself answers to the questions: "Who am I?" and "Where am I going?"

"I am the one who will restore a democratic government in my country and bring reforms to make my people's life easier".

Benazir worked hard, both emotionally and mentally, to get her mission accomplished. She demonstrated great courage being persecuted, repressed and imprisoned. Every single day she lived for her goal, doing everything she could for the well-being of her country.

She organized nationalization of oil deposits and directed cash flows to the implementation of social programs. As a result of her reforms, illiteracy among people of the country was reduced by one-third, the epidemic of poliomyelitis was averted; poor villages were connected to electricity and drinking water supplies. In addition, she introduced free healthcare and education and increased budget expenses for these purposes. During the time of her administration, the total volume of external investments increased several times, and the economic development rate in Pakistan was higher than in the neighboring India. These reforms of Benazir Bhutto were highly evaluated not only by Pakistani people but across the globe.

In 1996 she was included in the Guinness Book of Records as the most popular international politician of the year. She was granted an Honorary Doctorate Degree from Oxford University, a French Order of the Legion of Honor and many other awards.

Knowing the purpose of her life, she managed to introduce reforms in education, medicine and government institutions. She worked every day to the peak of her capacity to fulfill her purpose. She conducted many reforms in her country; the people of Pakistan literally worshiped her. Knowing the purpose of her life, she tromped through many difficulties and overcame hindrances.

On 27 December 2007, Bhutto became a victim of another terrorist attack in the city of Rawalpindi where she spoke at the meeting before her supporters. After the meeting, a suicide bomber shot her in the neck and chest and activated an explosive device. Bhutto was rushed to the hospital with serious injuries and she died on the operating table without regaining consciousness.

In the destiny of this woman, we can see a strong devotion to the main goal of restoring democracy in her country; she made huge efforts, spent inner and intellectual resources to take her people to a higher level of life and to build a public government on the principles of democracy. Devotion to the goal, knowing herself and her purpose, helped her go through pain, hindrances, crisis, and imprisonment. She was not afraid of terrorist attacks and she became the most influential woman in Pakistan as well as a well-known politician in the world. She was the first woman to be elected as the head of an Islamic state government.

This is how the world community valued her achievements:

- United Nations Human Rights Award
- Liberal International Prize for Freedom (1989)
- Academy of Achievement Award (2000)
- A member of Phi Beta Kappa society.

Great people have goals and achieve them.

It is important to know: goals must be formulated. It is better to break them down into parts, and then think over the plan of their implementation. Then you must consciously and carefully write out a plan of achieving your goal. Why must you do it this way? Your consciousness, which is responsible for decision-making and goal-setting, will give your subconsciousness problems to solve. So your subconsciousness will work to solve them.

That's why you need to write down your goals and plans.

1. Having defined your purpose and mission:
   - You need to implement the program directly concerned with your goals every day.

Each of us must have something to live for: one point, one phrase.
   - Set realistic terms for its implementation.

Great people become great due to the framework, routines and habits they have set for themselves.
   - Determine the actions you should do every day to achieve your goals.

Turn these actions into systematically repeated things, make them your routines.
   - Touch your goals every day. It means carrying out a part of the plan to reach your goals within the time limits you have set.

2. Remember that often we will not know the small details of our life mission. There is nothing to be afraid of in it. For example, today you may not know if you will be the Minister of Education. You may know that your calling lies in the field of education, but you may not know specifically if you are called to be a Minister of Education. You may know your life mission in general. Sometimes

the knowledge of "Where am I going?" comes during the process of implementation and dedication to the task. Sometimes it depends on the faithfulness in little things, for example, when you constantly devote your time to studying a certain topic, and sometimes you work on creation or implementation of your dream or idea, but you do not see your results immediately. You move gropingly, relying on your faith, and act by your intuition.

3. Even if you know where you are going and what problems you have to solve, you may only know the nearest tasks and you may not understand completely all of your tasks.

In order to answer the question "Where am I going?" one needs to work for self-improvement, to possess decisiveness, to have a will to win and dedication toward achieving the goal at all cost. It is necessary to grow up in maturity, firmness and courage in order to reach the goal.

On the other hand, the research process is very important. You need to study all things related to your goal. You need to study all the details of how you can achieve your goal. Learn your topic through self-study, through scrupulous analysis and learning about your goal. The deeper we dig into our field, the more we know about its details. We can find successful people in our field, learn from their experience and understand some important things more specifically. We need to go through all these processes in order to understand what our calling is.

4. In order to understand our life mission and answer the question "Where am I going?" we need to grow and shape our personality. This process is called self-realization or self-actualization. Maslow, one of the classic psychology authors, says:

"Self-actualization is also an ongoing process of discovering potential capacities. It suggests application of one's abilities and mind, as well as the "work for the sake of doing what you do in a good way. Great talent and reasonableness are not the same as self-actualization. Many gifted people could not use their abilities in full, while others who might have had only average talents did incredible things."

R. Freyger "Abraham Maslow and psychology of self-actualization." Psychology of a Personality. Collection of works, Moscow; Moscow State University, 1982. — 25 p.

"There is only one best way towards a good life for a man: try to be yourself more and more. Learn how to release the depressed, to research your inner self, to listen to the "voice of the impulse," to reveal your majestic nature, to reach understanding, penetration, to comprehend the truth — that's what it takes." A. Maslow. We need to get to know ourselves by discovering our special gifts and talents and unique traits of our personality.

"True self-realization happens only when we know ourselves, our own nature, and will realize it." (A. MASLOW)

Discussing this topic, the American Psychologist Frank Purls gives the example of an elephant and an eagle. Each of them has its own potential, which they implement in their lives. "They are what they are," he says. "How absurdly would an elephant look if it grew tired stomping its feet on the ground and wished to fly, gut rabbits and lay eggs. The same applies to an eagle who would want to possess the strength and thick skin of an elephant." Yes, these actions would be ridiculous for animals, but they are somehow acceptable for us. Instead of realizing ourselves, we are engaged in cloning others' lives.

American Psychologist Abraham Maslow says that the human need for self-actualization is just the desire to become what he can be, do things for which he was born. If the person does not satisfy the need for self-actualization, his dissatisfaction and anxiety increase.

The self-actualization process for a man is a conscious choice of a life goal and the way to achieve it. In this case, a person faces problems, accepts challenges and makes efforts to solve problems and implement his goals. Through solving problems, we improve and develop ourselves, reach maturity and strengthen our will. If we do not accept this challenge and remain in the comfort zone, then we undergo degradation.

The life of Mikhail Lomonosov is an example of a self-realized man, who achieved much thanks to his perseverance, the will to win, the ability to accept challenges and diligence. The life of Lomonosov is a good example of a man, who knows the answer to the question: "Where am I going?" and achieves his goal.

Born into a peasant family in a distant maritime European region, he was seemingly doomed to live as his ancestors lived. Instead, Lomonosov learned to read and write on his own and continue his education. Experiencing "indescribable poverty", the young man began to study at the Slavic-GreekLatin Academy, suffering mockery from his classmates, he still made good progress, finishing three courses of study within one year. Now being among the best students, he was sent to study in Germany, where he demonstrated his multifaceted interests, engaged in philosophy, physics, mathematics, mining and chemistry. It is astonishing to see his brilliant academic activities where scientific discoveries followed one another in almost all known sciences: astronomy and geography, geology and metallurgy, navigation and seafaring, history and art. Many of Lomonosov's ideas received scientific confirmation only 100 or 200 years later when scientists finally had the proper equipment to check his theories. Alexander Pushkin, the outstanding Russian poet, has rightly referred to Lomonosov as "our first university."

As we have seen in the example of Lomonosov, he knew the purpose of his life and reached it confidently. Neither lack of funds nor mockery of his classmates could stop him. He faced all challenges of life because he knew who he was, knew the purpose of his life and completely dedicated himself to it. Overcoming all obstacles, he improved himself, developed his natural abilities, with every problem making him only stronger.

Thus in achieving one's goals, one improves, develops and discovers his potential. If a person refuses to develop his potential, it can lead to nervous or mental disorders, somatic diseases and personal degradation. The absence of conditions for self-realization in a country, region and community leads to stagnation, the social and economic crisis there.

Let's make a conclusion: in order to answer the question "Where am I going?" you need to not only understand your mission, but also work at self-improvement; use your strong points and strengthen your weak points; engage in self-development, self-education, and development of will and firmness. This is a lifelong process.

5. It is important to study your mission, your goal. Permanent self-development and self-education are also very important. You must learn everything that can assist you in achieving your goals.

Personal development is "a development which depends on inner reasons, regardless of external factors."

Let us consider the issue of self-development in the example of Benjamin Franklin — a politician, diplomat, scientist, inventor, journalist and publisher. Benjamin Franklin loved books since his childhood, and he achieved much through reading, which promoted his continuous development and love of knowledge. Since the age of 16, he studied languages and philosophy — in particular, Socrates and Pythagoras, as well as rhetoric.

Franklin began working at his brother's printing works, but crippling work terms forced him to find a way to terminate his contract. When the contract was terminated, Franklin could not find any job in his city because his brother had visited all other printers and persuaded them not to hire Franklin.

But, as we said above, the man who has a goal does not stop when facing obstacles, rather he overcomes them thus improving himself. Franklin went to another state to be as far away as possible from his relatives.

Through hard work and a responsible approach, the young Franklin turned out to know the printing business better than most renowned printers.

As we can see, Franklin, knowing his vocation and thanks to self- education, managed to be the best in printing at the age of eighteen years. He was better than all printing works owners who were older and more experienced than him. Thus he was able to settle well in Philadelphia and was known as the best expert in this field.

Success in work and writing articles that he sometimes managed to publish allowed him to make friends with the local governor. He persuaded Benjamin to go to Britain in order to bring back equipment for a new printing works and promised his financial support. However, he went back on his promises and Franklin had to live and work in London for eighteen months. Despite this difficult circumstance, Benjamin Franklin managed to gain even more experience by working there.

A man going straight towards his goal overcomes difficulties and obstacles in his path, and turns them into benefits; he turns challenges into opportunities and improves himself through overcoming obstacles.

When he was 20, he came back to Philadelphia again, where he learned the principles of doing business and financial reporting. Even in his early age, his previous employers invited him to work as a printing works manager. He soon joined one of his colleagues as a partner and started his own printing press.

About a year before, Franklin and his friends had founded a club for joint development, where they met regularly and shared useful ideas. They prepared reports on interesting topics, exchanged books, and years later this secret club would prepare drafts of new bills. There, Benjamin Franklin was able to get the first orders for his printing works thanks to new connections and acquaintances.

We can see how important self-development is. Knowing his purpose helped Franklin use all available resources in favor of his goal, and the club also became an opportunity. Franklin used the club as leverage to launch his business and his political career.

In a short time, Franklin was already publishing his own newspaper, printed paper money for the government, and fulfilled other big orders — in many aspects it was thanks to his superior work quality which was visible to the naked eye when compared to his competitors. In addition, his public activities helped him make friends with future customers.

In his papers, he published articles about important social projects and, together with his friends from the club, he got interested in the government and ordinary citizens. As a result of his efforts, roads were paved with cobblestones, municipal street cleaners appeared in cities, and the streets were now lit. It sounds impressive, not to mention all kinds of inventions, such as heating systems. Finally, he helped raise funds to create the first municipal hospital, build a church and was one of the founders of the public school, which later grew up into the University of Philadelphia.

We can see tremendous progress in Franklin's life. He knew who he was; he knew his mission and educated himself in his field. He became not just an owner of the printing works, but also a writer, social activist, author of bills and the founder of the University.

Contrary to the widespread belief that only U.S. Presidents are pictured on American paper money, Franklin was never a president of the United States, but only a modest President of the Supreme Executive Council of Pennsylvania and one of the Founding Fathers who signed the Declaration of Independence in 1776 (as a representative from the UK). However, even these historic achievements are enough for his life principles, a way of thinking, willingness to work and his perseverance to become an example for many people of different generations. The sooner we find the answer to the question "Where am I going?" the greater results in life we can achieve.

6. In order to fulfill our life mission, we also need to develop perseverance, because even if we answer the question: "Where am I going?" without perseverance, we will not be able to achieve our goal. So, to achieve our goals, we need:

- Perseverance
- Persistence
- Tenacity

These are some of the most important qualities one must have to be successful in life and become realized.

Persistence and tenacity are important components of a unique individual. Without them, we are like animals and become a "gray mass."

The absence of these qualities in a person's character is the same as a man without a spine.

> *"Perseverance is a hard work you do after you get tired of doing the hard work you have already done."* (NEWT GINGRICH, AN AMERICAN POLITICIAN)

Will includes perseverance, persistence and tenacity.

If one of these three qualities is absent, then the will of a man is ill and weak.

If a person has a strong will, he always has initiative and is proactive. Pro-activeness is the ability to:

- actively set goals and find means to achieve them;
- subject one's thoughts, feelings and actions to this goal;
- show initiative.

Features of persistence:

- Backbone: the ability to show the will and character in defending one's position.
- Diligence: willingness for work and persistence.

Nothing in the world can take the place of persistence. Talent will not; nothing is more common than unsuccessful talented men. Genius will not; unrewarded genius is almost a proverbial thing. Education will not; the world is full of educated derelicts.

"Persistence and determination alone are omnipotent. The slogan "Press On!" has solved problems before and will always solve problems of the human race." Calvin Coolidge, 30th President of the United States.

Thus: only perseverance and decisiveness are omnipotent.

- Decisiveness

Courage and confidence

Ability to make and implement quick, well-grounded and firm decisions.

- Persistence

It is a trait of character, expressed in perseverance, persistence, striving to achieve the goal, at any cost and despite the obstacles.

- Constancy

As a part of persistence is an ability to endure and to be firm. It is also a firm devotion to one's beliefs and views.

"When I look at the stone cutter hammering away at a rock for a hundred times without so much as a crack showing in it but splitting the rock in two with the 101st blow, I think that it was not the last blow that did it, but the total of all blows his hammer done before." Jacob Riis, an American photographer.

Due to persistence and perseverance, Thomas Edison, the world-famous American inventor and entrepreneur, invented the light bulb in spite of many failed attempts and became a scientist of world renown.

Mozart, while still a three-year child, played piano and began to write his own music. He did it persistently all his life.

Later he became a composer of world renown.

When asked how he manages to write such works, Bach said: *"If everyone worked as much as I did, they would have achieved the same results."*

His answer showed that persistence and hard work are an integral part of any success.

"It's not that I'm so smart, it's just that I work on problems longer."

Albert Einstein, one of the founders of modern theoretical physics.

TENACITY AND PERSEVERANCE ARE THE GREATEST WORK

Everyone can give up. It is the simplest way to solving a problem. If you're tired, have a rest, then continue to move toward your goal; show tenacity, perseverance and persistence. Having achieved the desired result in the end, you will see it for yourself: "It was worth it."

Make a decision for yourself: "You must win the race!"

"The highest distinguishing feature of man is perseverance in overcoming the most difficult obstacles."

Ludwig van Beethoven, a German composer and pianist.

Never Give Up. After a late night, morning always comes. Therefore, when it seems that there is no way out, always remember — the morning will come.

If we show perseverance, the laws of the universe will work in our favor.

"Stable psychology is when life breaks its leg while kicking you." (A FOLK WISDOM)

I cannot help citing an instance of an amazing man called Alex who lost his legs during a practice mountain tour. Alex broke both his legs and got them frostbitten in 2009 during a training mountaineering tour of Elbrus. Yet in two years he could ski as well as walk and work.

This person did not give up and in spite of being without legs, he could accomplish more than healthy and full-bodied people. This story is about a courageous man who managed to mobilize all his strength, energy and spirit and fulfilled his destination, achieved his purpose and dream despite the amputation of both legs. He could have drowned in despair, stopped and given up. However, Alex took advantage of this formidable obstacle in order to become a true man of the spirit and encourage people by his example.

Alex began training and started to be engaged in serious competitions only two years after this serious injury and today, sports is a major part of his life. He managed to come in third at the winter sports Olympic — he was outrun by two competitors without fingers on their hands.

As you see, if a person is aware of his destination, life target and true being, neither injuries nor state of health will stop him. As it turns out, a person can be a champion even without legs.

What is the meaning of your life? What gives you the reason to live?

For me, the reason to live lies in internal confidence. I am not willing to express my opinion using scriptural phrases, but nevertheless, they are more accurate: "Each of us was created in God's kinship and similarity." It is always essential to feel and know it. If a man realizes this information, all obstacles will be perceived as ordinary work that has to be done.

Do you see what significance, good self-appraisal and correct self-identification can have? Alex reaches his goals and carries out his destination primarily through sound self-esteem.

Love has the most valuable meaning for me now. I understand it sounds terrible, but it is so. Moreover, the definition of love is not limited by the relationship between people. If a man does not love his work, he will definitely lose. Looking at a tree, we can see thousands of special features of it such as millions of leaves, branches and bark. However, the tree also contains something more than that; a tree has a kind of beauty. It is nothing more than a kind of unnatural idealized light but having a chance to see it proves the existence of love for the surrounding world. The moment it disappears everything is lost.

Alex overcame himself, won the struggle with his disability and did not lose faith in his life and destiny. His injury did not stop him, so he kept moving towards his target and dream. He was full of energy and enthusiasm. His soul and spirit are healthier than ours, while we are not disabled people. He does not stop to live his life in spite of all obstacles facing him. Indeed, he does not look at the problems; he set his heart on victory and new opportunities. He decided never to give up and to move ahead with confidence. Let's learn how to be steady and brave, assertive and obstinate, or how to have a will-to-win spirit using the patterns of life from such people.

PERSEVERANCE IS REWARDED

A person requires a lot of time to find a clue to baffling problems and a bit more time to complete what seems impossible. The last key in a whole bunch of keys opens the door.

If a person has a desire to go on to the next stage, he should not merely work more; he must do more than he did yesterday.

WE ARE PEOPLE OF UNLIMITED POSSIBILITIES

Applying maximum perseverance and maximum time you will be able to:

- conquer any city
- solve any problem
- make any dream come true

You only need to decide to sacrifice your time and a maximum of your strength (potential).

EVERYTHING WILL BE DONE, BUT NOT IMMEDIATELY

It is a mistake to think that anything you begin to do should always be all right from the first attempt. Be ready to face a failure, but remember: we can do anything!

Do not let fear take away your time by thoughts like "Nothing will come of it," "I cannot do it" and so on.

"With an ordinary talent and extraordinary perseverance, all things are possible." (THOMAS FOWELL BUXTON, AN ENGLISH POLITICIAN AND PUBLIC FIGURE)

CONCLUSIONS

1. You must clearly determine the purpose of your life. Every person should have a mission and goal, a point or a phrase to live for.

2. You must set and identify the real-time limits for its implementation.

3. You must decide what actions should be taken daily to reach your goals within the terms you have set for them.

4. You must get in touch with your purpose by doing a fixed amount of work every day.

5. You may not know from the very start all about your calling, but at the same time, you may be aware of the direction or field of it. Move on!

6. You must work to improve yourself; develop your individual traits in order to reach your target. It is a kind of self-education.

7. You must study your topic with great care.

8. You must develop perseverance, will and persistence in your character.

THE GOLDEN NUGGETS

1. When setting a goal our body starts to:

    - produce internal energy independently
    - mobilize all the strength in one direction It is our Creator's intention to provide us with the easier attainment of our goals.

2. A man must work on himself, his resolution and will-to-win spirit, grow in maturity, endurance and courage in order to answer the question "Where am I going?" Moreover, these traits can assist us to reach our goal.

3. A man must grow up as his own person and shape his character in order to identify his destination and goal, and answer the question "Where am I going?" This process is called self-actualization.

4. Refusing realization of one's potential can lead a person to many nervous and mental disorders, somatic diseases and degradation of personality. A region or community with no proper conditions for self-actualization breeds standstill, the social and economic crisis in the whole country.

5. What is most essential in achieving a set goal?

    - Perseverance
    - Steadfastness
    - Persistence

All these traits are extremely important and they should be put on the list of must-have traits for people who want to attain success and actualize themselves.

6. A person should seriously work on himself,

expend a lot of internal emotional and intellectual resources, and exert every effort to achieve the goal. He should be willing to work for 18 hours per day in order to attain mastery of his field, in order to fulfill his destination and achieve his purpose.

7. A starting point of self-foundation as a unique individual will appear in your life after clear determination of your goals.

TEST: ARE YOU AWARE OF THE PURPOSE OF YOUR LIFE?

1. **Are you engaged in self-education?**
   a) No, I have already graduated from an educational establishment (0)
   b) Sometimes, when I am keen on a topic (1)
   c) I am engaged in self-education every single day (2)

2. **Do you consider the purpose of your life to consist in going to school, graduating from a university or a post-graduate course?**
   a) Yes, it is essential for me (0)
   b) Schooling is important but in the field I am keen in (1)
   c) I need education only as a ground of achieving my purpose (2)

3. **Is creating a family one of the major purpose in your life?**
   a) Surely, it is essential for every human being (0)
   b) It is necessary to have a family as well as realize oneself in life (1)
   c) I indulge in actualization of my destination which brings satisfaction to me (2)

4. **Do you always have an active consciousness?**
   a) I become disconnected during conversations and boring meetings very frequently (0)
   b) I do my best to control myself and be here and now, but sometimes I fail (1)
   c) I always have an active consciousness (2)

5. **Can you work hard for 16–18 hours per day with a purpose of reaching your goal?**

    a) No, I need rest (0)

    b) Sometimes I can even be active all the night during a contingency or when I should meet the tight schedule (1)

    c) I can work for 16–18 hours per day with a purpose of reaching my goal (2)

6. **Have you already made a painstaking and scrupulous investigation of your target?**

    a) No, I have had no time for this (0)

    b) I studied my topic, but not very thoroughly (1)

    c) I investigated my topic thoroughly and scrupulously from top to bottom (2)

7. **Do you have such traits as perseverance, tenacity and persistence?**

    a) No, such traits are not developed in my character (0)

    b) These traits partly have a place in my life, but I should keep on developing them (1)

    c) Yes, these traits are well-developed in my character (2)

Test Results

0–4 points — We regret, but you have not asked yourself the question "Where am I going?" yet. You should not depreciate yourself. You should not consider yourself to be a small element in the corporate body. You have a potential, you were created for one essential target and you should identify it in order to be content with your life.

5–9 points — You are looking for your true being, but do not show sufficient perseverance in searching the purpose of your life. You should learn how to be in an active consciousness state, be here and now and answer the question "Who am I?" as well as build an inner system of values and beliefs. Leave your comfort zone; believe in yourself, your gifts and you will be satisfied with your life and capable of realizing your potential.

9–12 points — We are happy for you! You are aware of who you are and where you are going. You are a person of mature mind. You have worked on yourself and now you are approaching your goal and fulfilling your destination.

PRACTICAL TASKS

1. **Write down the time of achieving your purpose as exactly as possible.** If you are fond of painting, you can also depict it this way.

2. **Reflect on it and write down a purpose that you are moving toward.** Perhaps you are going in the wrong direction. Mark your position on your drawing.

3. **Will you be able to reach your destination in time advancing with such speed?** Will you have enough forces to maintain the chosen speed? If you should hasten your pace, how can you do this?

4. **Dwell on the things that make you closer to your purpose or, on the contrary, which take you away from it.** What should you do in order to concentrate on the most essential things in your life?

5. **The following exercises will help you to answer the question "Where am I going?"**

6. **The best day in my life!** Every one dreams of having an ideal life. What does having ideal life mean for you? What do you want to be engaged in everyday? In 10yrs, your ideal life should be realized and happen.

7. **The best year in my life!** Describe your ideal way of living. What will you be occupied with? Describe in details your ideal day, week, month, your meetings, trips, office life etc.

Recommended reading

||||||||||||||||||||||||||||||||||||||||||||||||||||||||||||||||||||||||||||||

I advise you to read the book "Why people fail to reach set targets?" by "The University of Life" in order to study this topic better.

CHAPTER 6

THE SYSTEM OF VALUES AND BELIEFS

THE SYSTEM OF VALUES AND BELIEFS

"Watch your thoughts; they become words. Watch your words; they become actions. Watch your actions; they become habits. Watch your habits; they become your character. Watch your character; it becomes your destiny." (ANONYMOUS)

Dear reader! Having read the previous chapters of this book, you have probably asked yourself a question: "What should I do in case I have not answered the question "Who am I?" yet and I am not yet aware of the purpose of my coming to the planet Earth?"

I suppose that you can become confused about it because you have already realized the importance of finding answers to these essential questions.

We put this chapter in the book for your special benefit. Read it attentively. Put everything that you will learn in this chapter into practice and the result will soon come.

Let's discern the main features of forming your "I" and personality based on your inner system of values and beliefs.

You should identify ten of the most essential life values and prioritize them accordingly: from the most important to the least important.

What does the phrase "life value" really mean?

Your inner core, values and beliefs, that create a ground for your life, make you a human being.

The choice of your values and the procedure of determining their importance take precedence over setting goals because values will be your reference point during your selection of goals. For example, you consider love and devotion to people to be your value but at the same time, you determine your destination as a businessman. Notice that you will have disagreements with your own mind because of discrepancies between your purpose and life values. Carrying on a business of your affairs will take up all the time devoted to creating your project; it will be your first consideration and you will have very little time for your family not to mention communication with people. The vocation of a clergyman serving in a local church or a coach holding self-development training with a purpose of realizing people's potential will be more suited for people with such values. Now you understand that being knowledgeable about your life values is extremely important.

I would like to cite some values as an example: God, vocation, family, health, destination, persistence, career, honesty, courage, love, gladness, relationship, creativity, success, passion, health, self-education, service to people, freedom, friends, security, etc.

Values are a force that is meant to push us forward; we make decisions that lead us to our goals in concordance with our life values. You come to a conclusion and take actions on the grounds of your life values. How else can you find them out? You should analyze what actions you have had previously.

We must derive a system of things that we appreciate most and consider them as the highest values, and then it is essential to live according to them every single day. Unfortunately, only a small group of people in our modern society manifest a desire to act in such a way. Very often people do not have even the slightest idea of the most essential things in their life.

How can we confront immense hassles, endure temporal inconveniences, overcome formidable obstacles and achieve our goals, if we are not able to picture the most essential thing in our life that we are ready to stand for under any circumstances?

Academician Sakharov stood alone against the society when the government decided to send Soviet troops to Afghanistan. He could not betray his values and beliefs. That is why he was not frightened of repressions and persecutions defending his point of view.

Ignorance of your values prevents us from making correct decisions. We must remember that all decisions taken are derived from a clear realization of our values.

For example, if you consider honesty to be one of your values, then even if you are offered a good deal which would go against your conscience, you will not consent to this offer; you won't hesitate on making the correct choice.

When you are aware of what is of value and importance to you, making a decision will obviously be a very simple thing to do. However, most people do not have a clear picture of things that are important in their lives and as a result, it is so difficult for them to take decisions.

People who know their values and live accordingly become leaders of society. We must clearly realize the most significant value in our life and make a decision to live in accordance with it, regardless of life circumstances. We should stick to our values in spite of them being approved or criticized. People following their principles and beliefs are admired and respected in our society. All of us have a profound respect for people who uphold their point of view and express undisguised support to their beliefs even when someone does not share their opinion.

Martin Luther King was an American clergyman, activist and a well-known leader of the African-American civil rights movement.

His greatest achievement is considered to be providing people with progress in the field of civil rights in the United States. He became a hero of the civil rights movement in America and fought for human rights throughout the entire world.

Martin Luther King was a pastor of a Baptist church. Being a Baptist clergyman, King started his struggle for civil rights, against racism and for social changes through exceptionally non-violent methods.

As a man of great spiritual power, he headed the Civil Rights Movement in the USA in the 1950–1960s.

He became a leader of the bus boycott caused by the arrest of the African-American woman, Rosa Parks, for her refusal to give up a seat on a bus.

The boycott continued for more than a year. A bomb was planted in King's house but he endured pressure and gained national recognition and great prestige as a leader of the civil rights movement.

We see in Dr. King an example of a person standing up for his values and beliefs. Menace did not quash his feelings; the assassination attempt did not intimidate him. His name remains in the country's history and today, he is known and recognized throughout the entire world. He did not live for a trifle; his life had an impact on many other lives and even changed the current legislation of the USA. It happened this way because he was not ignorant of his true being and the purpose of his birth. He also had his own system of values and beliefs and inner strength and stood up for it. At the age of 35, King received the Nobel Peace Prize, becoming the youngest laureate of this award in history.

King's defense of his beliefs ignited public opinion and made it possible to pass a number of laws by the U.S. Congress, which set a landmark in the struggle for equality: The Civil Rights Act, the Copyright Act, the Fair Employment and Housing Act.

"I have a dream that one day this nation will rise up and live out the true meaning of its creed: "We hold these truths to be self-evident, that all men are created equal." Awards:

- Man of the year 1963 (Time)
- the Nobel Peace Prize laureate — 1964
- Margaret Sanger Prize — 1966
- Presidential Medal of Freedom — 1977 (posthumously)
- Congressional Gold Medal — 2004 (posthumously)

King was aware of his true being and the purpose of his birth, he had the system of values and beliefs and the inner spirit to stand up for them!

His life is an example of how much can be changed by a single person, who is a uniquely self-actualized person capable of defending his own values and beliefs. He defends them despite the pressures of society and does not compromise them when facing difficulties.

Living in accordance with your positive values and beliefs is considered to be the only way to actualize yourself, fulfill your destination and be full of life energy. Otherwise, we will have to suffer.

You can ruin your inner peace when you choose to not align with your positive values. Taking a compromise, we feel frustration and inner emptiness.

Rose had a dream to become a lawyer. She was inspired to pursue this vocation after she witnessed a brilliant performance of a prominent lawyer in court. His touching speech did not leave anyone indifferent. He helped to acquit an innocent man who could be imprisoned unlawfully.

Considering her love for people and desire to make a contribution to their lives to be the most significant values, Rose made up her mind to become a lawyer. After some time passed, she found herself in the maelstrom of law practice. She learned many things and then she opened her own business and became head of her own law firm.

The field of her work changed and acquired a completely different direction. As a successful manager, she became one of the most prosperous women. However, she did not feel happy because of lack of communication with her clients. Her current position obliged her to maintain different connections with businessmen and she spent all her time attending meetings, conferences and making protocols. She reached a high position in society but she did not live in concordance with her life values. As a result, she felt disillusionment despite the success she achieved in her career.

We should create a system of values and beliefs in order not to feel frustration in our life. We try to suppress our feeling of dissatisfaction by things that can alter rapidly our state of mind. We begin to habitually watch television for hours; we eat and drink with the purpose of filling our inner emptiness, we control everything and give orders to others.

To live in concordance with our highest values is like a 'horse of a different color'; we experience an incredible feeling of enthusiasm. In this case, we do not need any surplus of water and food, time spent in front of the television, or empty conversations. We do not need to confuse ourselves because our life is bright and interesting in itself.

People set their goals without a clear understanding of what they really value, what is the most important thing for them, what things they will struggle for, what things they will defend, and soon they end up disillusioned with their lives after they have achieved their goals.

For example, you consider love to be your life value, but you are occupied with paperwork where you do not have any opportunity to help people and take part in their life. You can make a good career but if you abandon your values, you will suffer.

IN ORDER TO FIND OUT YOUR LIFE VALUES, YOU NEED TO:

1. Identify what current values you have and arrange them from the most essential to the least significant one. Prove to yourself why the chosen values are important.

2. Think of values on your list which must be changed in order for you to become a man you dream to be. "What values should I have in order to be capable of reaching the destiny that I wish to have and deserve to have?"

3. Write down a list of things that you want to avoid in your life. For example, it can be rejection, failure, disappointment, loneliness, fear of failure. You can compare your values with the picture of the person you want to become. For instance, your value is to achieve

success in life and what you want to avoid by all means is rejection, criticism and fear of failure.

You understand that it will not lead to success because your brain and your subconscious mind will be an obstacle to your moving forward on the account of fear of rejection, criticism and failure. You will suffer criticism, rejections and refusals on your way leading to success in order to achieve something in life. In this case, you should understand which of these unpleasant things you ought to refuse. Courage should become your new value.

You should conscientiously create your system of values and beliefs which corresponds to your ideal image of "I." You have a system of values that is built inside of you. Whatever happens to your body, it will not have any connection with your core values. A woman can be very attractive but unable to save her family. Her beauty cannot help her save a marriage, except for the honeymoon period.

If you are empty with no values inside or no core, men can choose you, and your body can temporarily get married. Your beautiful body does not mean anything about your true being. As time passes, this narrow-minded man who got married to a woman with a yet unformed identity will open his eyes and quickly see that there is no individuality inside the body of his wife — she is empty inside. Who should he continue to build relations with? So, this is how relationships break down and divorce comes.

Your body can be beautiful or ugly, thin or fat, but your true self is your inner content, your values, the truth you have built inside you, this is a system of truths and beliefs that determine the man's inner being. The core built in your soul consists of values, beliefs and truth.

WHAT IS A BELIEF?

Belief is a feeling of confidence regarding whatever there is. For example, if you consider yourself to be a person with a logical type of thinking, it would be the same way as if you claimed: "I am confident. I am a person with a logical type of thinking." This confidence allows you to use your internal resources to achieve the results you want.

For example, you think that you are attractive, so you say "I am confident that I am a beautiful woman."

When you consider yourself to be a gifted writer, it is equivalent to words: "I am confident I can write marvelous books that will alter the way people think." Your belief and confidence will draw up additional inner resources in your body in order to ensure that your belief is realized in this life. If you are not sure enough about your beliefs, you will not be able to use all of your inner capacity and resources.

So, if you really believe that you are a great writer, all internal resources will be used in order to help you to achieve the result you believe in and the world will know of your amazing ability to write books. The more you believe, the more resources you use.

Thoughts are the building materials for belief. You can have millions of thoughts but never believe in them.

For example, you claim "I am a talented writer", but if you think: "There are so many others out there better than I am. I am not really that gifted" at the same time, it means that you do not believe in this talent. You need to justify and prove every belief you have.

You should receive a confirmation of your thought in order to make a reality of it and have it become your belief. You have certain evidence to support these thoughts — certain life experiences that support them. What experience do you have to confirm it? Perhaps, one of your friends or teachers told you once that you have a good manner of writing or you understood that your texts are better while reading compositions by others authors, or editors praised your novels. All of these do not matter until you compose these statements into one idea that you are a gifted writer. Only in this case will your thought find confidence and will become your belief.

Every point needs to be justified:

- Why is it an advantage to me?
- How can it be useful to me?

You can create positive beliefs about life, people around you, and your goal in the same way as you created a belief of your being a gifted writer.

Then, should you focus your thoughts on this reality.

Later you will start to create this reality formed in concordance with your beliefs.

Beliefs can be positive or negative.

Each of us must identify negative beliefs that restrict our mind and get rid of them as soon as possible. For example, you say: I am a loser; no one was rich in our family, so I will not be; people treat me with hostility; never trust anyone; life is a difficult thing; it is difficult to rise above the crowd; people around me do not love me etc.

Global beliefs are considered to be strong beliefs concerning everything that makes up our life: your personality, people, work, time, money, and life in itself. These beliefs usually use the verb "to be": "Life is...", "People are representatives of..." Global beliefs can form our outlook, understanding of life and surroundings, and patterns of behavior. Having changed just one restricting belief, you will be able to change your life in a flash!

When they strike roots, beliefs become incontestable orders that are sent into our nervous system. They have a power of expanding our abilities and self-confidence or destroy the opportunities of our present and future. If you want to control your life, you must exercise conscious control over your beliefs and values.

Now we understand how beliefs are formed and how they can be changed. We are responsible to consciously form beliefs. We must find enough confirmations in order to justify our beliefs.

A person should be actively forming a vision of life, his values and beliefs — the stage of one's active conscience — long before he is 18 years old. Passing through periods of maturity, we must form our values. A foundation, a core leading us throughout all future life must be formed before we are 18yrs.

However, people sometimes cannot form their core because, after a period of rebellion and revolts (juvenile age), they fall under the influence of society. For example, instead of obeying his mother, the child begins to listen to friend's advice. Some people continue living at the level of reflexes and emotions, and act as everyone acts and never becomes the person that they were destined to become.

Sam grew up a sociable and communicative guy. His parents were busy working from morning till night to enable their son to study at a prestigious school and live in a home full of conveniences. Sam's parents prepared him to study at the university. They were happy to see their son's destiny different from theirs. They had to toil hard to earn money for an apartment in the capital. Having come from the country, they had to make a tremendous effort to get accustomed to being in a big city.

They planned a different destiny for Sam; he should have no problems because his parents tried so hard to give him a comfortable life, filled with many things.

Suddenly, the troubles began. One day, Sam returned home in a state of drug intoxication. Returning to his senses, he confessed he had been taking drugs for over a year. His school friends offered him drugs and he could not refuse because they were his best friends. His parents were too busy building a financial welfare and were not engaged in the creation of their son's inner core.

Sam's life was planned in advance for him. This plan was compiled by his family and not by him. He was to study at the university and later work for his father's firm. Sam had not thought of the purpose of his life. He was not aware of whom he was. Consequently, he did not have a system of life values and beliefs that were able to serve as an anchor for him in his life, values which would not let him swerve from the chosen path and would help him fulfill his life's destination. If he had determined his life plan, he would not have deviated from his purpose or wasted time on drugs and friends.

He did not choose a purpose to live for. Above all, he did not reflect on his life values and did not have an inner "anchor." That is why he was trapped by the drugs so easily. As a result, he spoiled his own life through his own actions. Presently, he took a drug treatment course. Sam will have to do enormous work to strengthen his will, create an inner core in order to get rid of his drug addiction and become a full-rate member of society. He should realize his goals in life and understand what he lives for. It will be a long and difficult journey with ups and downs. Let's hope Sam will be able to answer the question

"Who am I?" and determine the destination of his life, develop himself and his will in order to break free from drug addiction. A lot of time, power and energy will be lost. He will have to rebuild his life.

If Sam had built a system of values and beliefs, he would not have suffered in such a way. A person should have his system of values and beliefs built before he is 18yrs in order to be capable of directing his life independently. A man with an inner core cannot be influenced by society; nobody can have an impact on his decisions and actions.

You can understand from this example how important it is to build core and right values on a solid foundation so no one can influence anything in your life. If Sam had formed an inner anchor and his values consisted in, for example, fulfilling his destiny or achieving a set goal, he would not have done such silly things and wasted time on foolish adventures that resulted in an immense failure of his development.

Life values will become a reference point for you that will lead you to your destiny and goal.

Life values will be an anchor helping you not to be blown away from the right direction after achieving your goal and fulfilling your destiny.

CONCLUSIONS

1. Now, dear reader, you are not your attractive body, not your job and not your social standing. You are a system of values and beliefs that you have formed inside.

2. Your life values are your reference points in your search of your life mission and calling.

3. You can independently form a correct system of values inside you, which will not let you step away from your goal; they will be your anchor to keep you on course when you achieve success.

4. You need to make a decision and make efforts to live in accordance with your life values, and then you will enter the list of leaders.

THE GOLDEN NUGGETS

1. Values are the power pushing us forward.

2. Based on our life values, we make decisions which lead us to our goals.

3. Belief is the feeling of confidence in whatever it is.

4. The one who knows his values and lives accordingly will become a leader of society.

5. Beliefs may be both positive and negative. For everyone, it is important to find the negative beliefs restricting our mind and get rid of them as soon as possible.

6. If we want to control our lives, we need to bring our beliefs and values under conscious control.

SELF-EXAMINATION TEST

1. **Have you made up a list of your life values?**
   a) No, I don't even know what you mean (0)
   b) I have read this chapter and realize I need to make my list — TODAY (1)
   c) Yes, I have life values and I live accordingly (2)

2. **Do you have beliefs?**
   a) I have no time for that (0)
   b) I am working on it now — TODAY (1)
   c) Yes, I have a system of values and beliefs (2)

3. **Have you found your negative and restricting beliefs?**
   a) No, it's the first time I have heard of them (0)
   b) I understand how important it is but I have not found them yet (1)
   c) Yes, I have determined the restricting beliefs in me and changed them (2)

4. **Do you work on creating an inner core?**
   a) No, I don't (0)
   b) Yes, I do but not regularly (1)
   c) I have formed my inner core and I keep on working on my character (2)

5. **Do you work to form values and beliefs in yourself?**
   a) No, I don't (0)
   b) Yes, I do sometimes (1)
   c) Yes, I believe that everyone has to form himself independently (2)

Test Results

0–4 points — We are sorry but you haven't formed a system of values and beliefs. In order to be able to answer the question "Who am I?" it is extremely important to determine your life values. Then your values will become your reference points in determining your life mission.

5–9 points — You understand the importance of having life values and beliefs. They are also important to answer the questions "Who am I" Where am I going?" You do not have a clear answer to these questions. Spare some time for yourself and determine your life values; then it will be easier for you to determine your goals.

9–12 points — We are glad for you! You have built an inner core and have a strong system of values and beliefs.

PRACTICAL TASKS

1. **Find out your current values and arrange them by their significance.**

2. **Prove to yourself why the chosen values are important for you.** Think of what values on your list could be changed in order to become what you plan to be. "What should my values be like for me to achieve the destiny which I want to have and which I deserve?"

3. **Make up a list of things you want to avoid in your life.** For example, denial, refusal, disappointment, loneliness, fear of loss, fear of failure.

Recommended reading

||||||||||||||||||||||||||||||||||||||||||||||||||||||||||||||||||||||||||||||

For a more detailed study of this topic I recommend to read the books "I am a person. Am I a personality?", "How to be here and now" and "There is a man, there is no man" by "The University of Life."

PART 2

Hello,

I am your most cherished dream, and this is my story...

I was born together with you, and I have been living all this time in your heart. In your childhood, we were as one. We both believed that nothing is impossible in this life.

I encouraged you as well as I could when you felt bad. When things were really hard I gave you hope and strength to go on and the meaning of life.

But the years went by. The older your heart became the less room it had for me.

Parents, teachers, and friends — nobody believed in me, and told you: "such things never happen," "come down to earth," "you should live like everyone else."

Gradually, their thoughts became your thoughts.

You can find lots of reasons not to notice me: "I am tired," "your time will come soon," or on the contrary, "I have to work too hard," "I will not be able to do it."

Yet sometimes you remember me. In such moments you feel your heart shrink with pain.

But you force your thoughts way from me. I understand this makes your life easier — living without thinking of the dream that never came true.

You may think about it as my last message for you. Though I still believe we can do it and everything will be all right.

Will you fight for me?

With love and faith in you,

Your DREAM

Dear reader!

In the first part of our book, we have answered very important questions such as "Who am I? What can I do? Why am I here? What am I doing here? Where am I going?"

In the second part of the book, we will study answers to the questions: "How to find oneself; Practical steps in implementing your vision; Specific steps from a dream to its fulfillment; How to go from A to Z; Practical steps to implementation of your vision".

I can assure you that having answered all questions and having done all practical assignments given in the second part of the book, you will drastically change the quality of your life. This is something never taught at school or at the university. Training sessions held on these topics cost thousands of dollars. But now you have the chance to get it all almost free. The most important thing is your desire to change your life and bring to life the craziest dream you ever had.

So let us begin.

1. Take a pen and a notepad and answer these questions honestly. Ask for help from your friends and people who are interested in you.

2. Think attentively and reflect before answering. Be sure that the answer represents what your soul feels.

    Do not write all questions at once, reflect on them, give a well-grounded answer to one question and only then go to another one. Try to make a conclusion before thinking on a new item.

3. In your answers, try to single out the most obvious and the brightest manifestation of your calling, potential and gift. There may be several of these. In order not to get confused it would be preferable to answer the questions

in the form of a scale. That is, if you like reading, specify with the help of a 10-point scale how important it is for you.

If you were locked in a room alone, what would you do — draw, read or study? That is, you have to give a point of preference to every activity. For example, you would read (6 points), and study (8 points). Then you will understand better what is more exciting for you.

Put aside anything that can disturb or distract you and concentrate on answering in accordance with your real desire.

Believe me now that you are engaged in the most important thing in your life — you are determining your purpose in life and your life mission!

CHAPTER 7

HOW TO FIND YOUR CALLING

HOW TO FIND YOUR CALLING

1. Calling is in our natural desires. We were created to be passionate about something.

Passion is what we are striving for; it consists in things that attract us. What do you like to do naturally?

> *"Calling is feeling yourself in the proper place."* (ANNA UVAROVA)

What is your desire? What fascinates you? What attracts you? What do you like doing? What is your internal passion?

Answer the following questions: What do I want to do most of all? What does my inner self, my soul strive for? What attracts me? What has attracted me since my childhood? What do I like doing in my free time? What is my hobby?

For example, some women like to put things in order and look after themselves. Others, on the contrary, do not like doing it, they like to sell and promote products or they like to work with number and digits. In this case, their calling can be that of a manager or an accountant. Also they can run their own beauty salons, invent a product for health and beauty, as Mary Kay did and became a founder of the eponymous cosmetics company.

Do you like to ask questions? Journalists and lawyers usually like to ask questions. Maybe you like to solve people's problems.

It is a mandatory feature for church pastors. Maybe you have an oratorical talent, a talent for public speaking. Then you can become a trainer, a coach or a politician. Someone who likes to draw can become like Salvador Dali. Someone who likes to play piano can become another Sebastian Bach. Someone who does not like to talk much may become a writer. Someone who likes to delve into the mechanisms or small details can become an engineer or an inventor.

If you have several talents, begin to develop one of them and then try developing another one.

"All human beings, without exception, are talented. Talents are different and need to be developed. Some were lucky to find themselves in a profession, and some were not." Maria Sharapova.

Let us examine another story of success to confirm the above statements.

"Tennis is what drives her mad. Forget everything that does not belong to the tennis field like posing for magazines and anything else. Yes, she is also doing it, but I can assure you, in comparison with tennis, she does not care much for such things. What she can do on the court is above all for her! Just look once more at her when she is training. She never stands in the middle of the court and never spends too much time for exercise. No, she goes onto the court and says, "Well, let's start, dam it!" She's a real fighter and anyone in the academy, who engages in a sparring with her, turns into a guinea pig very quickly," says Nick Bollettieri, the coach for Maria Sharapova.

Maria burst into the top twenty list of tennis players in 2004. First, Maria won the tournament in Birmingham in singles and doubles, and three weeks later she turned her dream into reality. On July 3, 2004, Maria won the Wimbledon tournament, having confidently, beautifully and daringly beaten the American Serena Williams in the final women's singles; just think about it — before that, Serena had been a double winner of this tournament. Thus Maria, who had been just a promising and talented player before, became the new bright star of the world tennis community.

On 4 April 2005 Maria became the leader of the WTA title race for the first time and on April 11, a week before she turned 18, she became the second best player in the world! At the annual ATP and WTA awards ceremony, held in Miami, Maria Sharapova took the first prize in three categories: "The best female tennis player 2004 by the WTA Tour," "The Most Advancing Player" and "The People's Choice Award." The Forbes magazine included Maria on the list of "Top 100 Most Influential Celebrities," and she was the only Russian woman on the list. In Los Angeles, Maria won the prestigious U.S. prize, ESPY Awards in 2004. She has been recognized by ESPN as the best female tennis player of the year.

Maria's greatest advantages are her willpower, mental firmness and a competitive spirit. She is a long-legged beautiful blonde, impressing everyone with her natural talent. She embodies the union of inner strength and beauty.

She was born on April 19, 1987, in Nyagan, a small town in Siberia. In 1989 her family moved to Sochi, a city on the Black Seashore. At the age of four, a random event had changed her life. A friend of her family gave her one of his son's tennis rackets. This gift ignited a passion for tennis in Maria. She started playing and could not stop it. Maria asked her parent to send her to a tennis academy because she could not think of anything other than tennis.

In this example, we can see the passion she developed for tennis. As a child, Maria opened her natural gift, understood her life calling and confidently went towards her aim. She gained recognition throughout the world and in her own country. Her natural talent and knowledge of her mission made her well-known and famous.

In 1993, the famous tennis player Martina Navratilova saw talent in Maria and approached Sharapova's father to allow her to begin the girl's training at the Tennis Academy in Florida.

When she was only 7 years old, Maria and her father moved to the United States with the purpose of entering the Tennis Academy of Nick Bollettieri.

IMG Sports Company agreed to be Maria's sponsor and provided her with a scholarship of $35,000 per year which she needed for training at the Academy. Her achievements now speak for themselves.

Now she is the winner of 28 WTA single tournaments, including four Grand Slam tournaments and three WTA doubles, as well as the 2004 Final Championship. The first racket of the world by the WTA Tour Ranking (total time spent in the first place is 21 weeks in 4 times): the first time at 18, from August 22 to September 12, 2005, and recently from June 11, 2012 to July 9, 2012.

Maria Sharapova was the most requested athlete in Yahoo search engine in 2005 and 2008. In July 2008 and 2010, as a result of her success on the court as well as outside it, she was recognized as the highest paid athlete in the world, with the annual earnings of $26 million. Since February 2007, she has been an ambassador of goodwill.

Because of her natural beauty, enthusiasm, passion and extremely loud cries, while hitting the ball, she was called "The Siberian Siren" or "The Queen of Screams."

Maria discovered her gift early. She found her calling and understood her destiny. The passion for tennis helped her to do it. As a result, she is effective in achieving her goals. She has completely realized herself, not only as an athlete but also as a fashion model. Her unique personality was discovered and now she is an inspiration to many people.

2. What would you love to do, even if you were not paid for it?

"If you do not like to do something for free, why do you think you will love this occupation for money? It does not matter if I am rich or not, I am happy, because I enjoy what I do. This is actually the main wealth."

Here is where your identity lies. Who are you?

What would you like to do with pleasure and joy? The answer to this question is your calling. It is what you should do. What would you still do, even if you did not get money for it? Write books, run the beauty industry, sell goods, establish companies?

3. What are you good at?

Write a list of things you are good at.

It is where you should look for your destiny, your gift. For example, you may be good at:

- cooking
- putting things in order
- noticing what is wrong
- chatting

- making friends
- being creative
- reading etc.

> *"Let everyone do what he under-stands best."* (MARCUSCICERO).

Someone is good at writing, someone is good at criticizing, someone is good at putting things in order and someone is good at cooking. Someone can build good relationships with people, someone likes to read and someone likes to sew. This is where your calling is hidden.

4. What gives you the most satisfaction?

When you are busy with this peculiar activity you:
- Feel good
- Experience happiness
- Feel joy

If a person does not get satisfaction and joy from what he does, his life is colorless. It leads to depression and mental disorders. The person feels himself just to be just a tiny element of a huge system. And he sees no sense in his life, finds no satisfaction. Continuing to live this way can lead to being a patient in a psychiatric hospital.

5. What do people notice in you?

What do people often give you compliments and praise you for?

What were you noticed and praised for in your childhood? Having become adults, we are now seen as rivals and competitors, and we get more criticism than praise. Try to think and remember what people noticed in you. This is where your calling, your identity, and your destiny may be.

> *"Everyone has his own specific calling. Everyone is irreplaceable, and his life is unique. Therefore the task of each person is as unique as his ability to perform this task."* (VIKTOR FRANKLE)

6. For what qualities in you do people like the most?

Refer to your colleagues, friends, neighbors and relatives:

- What do they love you for?
- What do they dislike in you?
- What did they like in you in your childhood?
- Why do they envy you?

What qualities make most people dislike or envy in you?

> *"Envy attacks the highest virtues and spares only mediocrities."* (GASTON DE LEVIS)

7. What makes you different from others?

- What makes me special and different from others?
- What were you criticized and ridiculed for?

In things where you are special and different from others, your largest uniqueness is hidden. Find something that makes you different from others. It will become your ADVANTAGE, your primary weapon.

"All great men have a common feature: they stood out against the colorless crowd. To really stand out, we just have to do what we love and can do best. After all, the love of our calling makes us different from others."

8. What can you do without preparation?

What naturally comes from you (I do not mean negative things but creative)?

You can do this:

- Unwittingly,
- Without preparation,
- Without motivation,
- On the run, spontaneously.

What can you do without preparation, on the run? Think, communicate, analyze, keep silent, smile. What do you do naturally? Smile, sing, write or improvise. Others need to force themselves into doing it, but you do it naturally. What are you good at naturally, without preparation, without training?

> *"Only scientists, and also the Greeks, are used to talking without preparation on a given topic."* (CICERO)

9. What can you do without noticing the time?

There are some things we can fully immerse ourselves into and become devoted to. This is something we can be busy with, without noticing the time. There are some things we do without lending our soul to the task. There are also some things you can immerse into with your head, your heart and your soul, and forget about time. What can you do without noticing time, without looking at the clock?

Let's remember Thomas Edison, Steve Jobs and Madonna: they are willing to do their work, forgetting about time, forgetting about everything.

10. What would you stay alone with?

If you were locked in a room for three days or a week and you could not go out, what would you have asked to take with you? What would you like to stay alone with?

- TV set
- The Internet
- Yourself
- Books
- Friends

What would you like to stay alone with and enjoy it?

11. What would you prefer to stay alone with?

"Loneliness is a natural refuge of all thoughts: it inspires all poets, it creates actors, and it inspires geniuses." (JEAN BATISTE HENRI LACORDAIRE)

"You do not need to leave you own room. Continue to sit at your desk and listen. You need not even listen, just wait. You need not even wait; just learn the mystery of calmness, stillness and solitude. Then the world freely appears before you in its undisguised form. It will not have a choice: it will roll in ecstasy at your feet." (FRANZ KAFKA.)

12. What do you like to read, listen, and talk about?

There are some topics you may like to read, listen and talk about most of all. Some people may like to talk about:

- weather
- charity
- children

- strategy
- books etc.

All these things may become a prompt for you.

What do you like to do — read or listen? What do you like to talk about: weather, salvation, children, or strategies?

Often we do not think about these things. What do you like, what are you fond of? Think about it. There are some topics you like to talk and listen about, and tell others about them.

13. What do you think about most often?

What do you think about most often?

> *"What a great calling it is to build the way for the obscure truths and new brave ideas."* (HENRIK IBSEN)

14. What could you do so intensely that you forget about meals?

What can get you carried away with so much that you might forget whether you had dinner or not?

> *"One's calling can be recognized and proved only by the sacrifice a scientist or an artist makes for his peace and well-being."* (LEO TOLSTOY)

What could get you so much carried away that you might completely forget about dinner, breakfast or food at all? And maybe even about sleep?

15. Who inspires you?

Who inspires you? We want to be like them and to be as successful as them.

- Make a list of people who inspire you.

- Categories of people who inspire you and whom you want to copy.

What kind of people do you admire? Are there people who inspire you, the people you would like to copy, and the people whose success makes you want to be as successful?

16. Where do your love and hate meet?

Where does your passion collide with your irritation? The thing you love very much or hate very much can be your calling.

For example, the family topic can raise ambivalent feelings in you. This topic concerns you; you cannot remain indifferent to it. On the other hand, this topic gives you pain and feelings that are associated with your divorce, because you had not been prepared for family life. Get to grips with it. This topic can be your calling. You have studied the topic of family deeply and understood that for a successful family life, you did not have enough training and knowledge. You have realized all your mistakes and shortcomings and made some conclusions. You want to use your knowledge and the experience you have gained in order to help those who only intend to enter into marriage. This is the area where your pain and your love meet.

> "I am proud to have been in a business that gives pleasure, creates beauty, and awakens our conscience, arouses compassion and perhaps most importantly, gives millions a time off from our so violent world." (AUDREY HEPBURN)

For example, you think, "I love my country; but on the other hand, when I see what's going on here it upsets me."

You learn public administration in other countries to bring positive lessons in this field for your country. You do not stay indifferent to everything that happens in the public administration of your country. You are ready to learn, change something in the economy and public institutions, and spend your time, energy, effort and all your intellectual and emotional resources.

17. Find books, literature and information regarding the abilities and gifts which are there in you.

The more we know, the deeper we will understand our topic, so it will be easier to implement it.

18. Find the right surroundings, the people who will help you to carry out your mission and realize your gift.

It is well-known that the environment determines 50 percent of our success. If you want to become a journalist, you need to communicate with journalists and professionals in this sphere. If you want to become an outstanding sales manager, you need to find appropriate surroundings and additionally attend training on sales. If you want to become a politician, enter the political surroundings. You will be surprised to see how many people have become politicians without having a calling for it. It happened just because someone had promoted them. They found themselves in the right place at the right time. You need to determine the field of your gift and enter into the realm of experts for that calling.

CHAPTER 8

THE PRINCIPLES OF FULFILLING DREAMS. HOW TO GO FROM A TO Z

THE PRINCIPLES OF FULFILLING DREAMS. HOW TO GO FROM A TO Z

"So many of our dreams at first seem impossible, then they seem improbable, and then, when we summon the will, they soon become inevitable." (CHRISTOPHER REEVE)

Widespread justifications formulate the most significant obstacles on the way to achieving a dream. Very frequently we only dream and do so because we do not know HOW to go from a dream to its fulfillment.

There are two major justifications given:

1. I do not know how — it is a question of process. You do not understand the process of achieving and fulfilling a dream;

2. I do not have any opportunities such as money and resources.

Both points are important for fulfilling your goals.

"A person always has everything to be capable of fulfilling his dream." (PAULO COELHO)

And now the most unbelievable thing!!!

We prepared answers and practical advice with the purpose of helping you to cope with obstacles on the way to achieving your dream.

1. **You must sit down and do a complete analysis which means:**

- To calm down

- Not to hurry

Usually, when people get an idea, they are eager to start acting immediately, immerse themselves in the process without creating a system of actions, without being knowledgeable of the matter, without analyzing and estimating everything beforehand. They do not reach planned results and lose heart only on this account.

Stopping, sitting down and finding time for reflection are considered to be the most essential action related to fulfilling a human's destination.

To sit down means to calm down without rush and fuss, stop and reflect, analyze all pros and cons, count all possible merits and faults.

2. **"Calculate expenses"**

This expression means to:

- Conduct a detailed investigation of this issue or a field you are interested in;

- Study this direction and find a maximum amount of information about this issue; read all possible information concerning it.

You should conduct a research — to study the issue or field you are interested in; explore the topic in every quarter and search information in all kinds of sources.

3.   The choice of information

- Something that you need in particular.

- Something that you prefer more.

Having collected enough information concerning your topic, you will be able to achieve your dream. The analysis is the next essential thing.

For instance, you are fond of sewing. You explored the marketing outlets and made a conclusion that it is better to sew winter clothes or, on the contrary, ladies' underwear. What things are in demand for that market? You should provide yourself with detailed information in order to identify the necessary range of production.

3.   You should build a system

"A goal without a plan is just a wish."
(ANTOINE DE SAINT-EXUPERY)

- A system should be viable. It should let your dream to be developed and born.

- The entire process must be divided into stages. EXAMPLE:

The stages of making clothes:

1. Analysis of market trends

2. Selection of color scale

3. Selection of fabric and accessories

4. Creation of sketches

5. Creation of a prototype model

6. Elaboration of garment cutout and model

7. Sewing of a prototype model

8. Creation of basic patterns

9. Sewing of the first batch of goods

10. Elaboration of technical documents

You should create a system or structure helping you to turn your dream into reality. It can be patterns or dress patterns for a tailor or cutter. Then you need to identify the sequence of stages: to design an item, create basic patterns, cut out the fabric and give it to the garment factory, create a technological process there, and find fabric, equipment, staff and the market.

4. **Create a structure**

Write down all details of your process from A to Z.

- Work out the details
- Every stage should contain answers and solutions Example: making pancakes. Plan:

1. Ingredients and products.

2. Frying pan

3. Kitchen — equipment

4. Cook

5. Relation

The procedure starts from the beginning of cooking. Every point should be written down specifically and precisely in order to make this plan structured. For example, seasoning is not suitable for this pattern. We need flour, powder, sugar, milk, eggs and butter to cook pancakes. Everything should be written down bottom-up; everything should be interconnected and interacted.

Example: opening a fitness club network.

1. You must form an idea.

2. You must conduct a research: how many coaches you need, what training equipment you need, and what sports programs you will offer to your visitors.

3. You must create a team

4. You must find a premise

5. You should buy equipment

You have a plan to open 1 fitness club within 3 months and duplicate it 4 times within a year.

The reality will be the following: 1 fitness-club in 2 months and 8 — in a year. Every stage must contain answers and solutions.

You should write down all process and provide:

1. Interaction and correlation between them

2. Cyclic recurrence

3. Closed loop

After that, you must begin a new stage called process. We start to correlate with all these stages and provide cyclic recurrence, connect one thing with another and close a loop. So, this is the procedure of process. The process is an interaction from A to Z without gaps.

"The soul of the sluggard craves and gets nothing." (SOLOMON — PROVERBS 13:4 ENGLISH STANDARD TRANSLATION)

CHAPTER 9

SPECIFIC STEPS FROM A DREAM TO ITS FULFILLMENT

SPECIFIC STEPS FROM A DREAM TO ITS FULFILLMENT

For the best illustration of this chapter, I would like to get you acquainted with Sara Blakely. I love this story for a lot of reasons: "It's entertaining, impressing and inspiring. In 2012, at the age of 41, Blakely became the youngest self-made woman to get onto the Forbes billionaire list.

Sara had an idea, created a prototype, set up manufacturing facilities, and invented the brand name. She designed the package and patented the product on her own. Sara organized photo sessions to demonstrate her invention on her own body. Blakely said she spent two years actually standing in department stores selling Spanx and talking to shoppers.

According to Forbes, Sara made incredible success without spending a single dollar on advertising. Her initial capital was only $5,000.

How did she manage to do it? The idea for Spanx first came to Sara Blakely in 1998. She was planning to wear a pair of white slacks and she worried that her panty lines would show through her pants. She opted for a do-it-yourself approach: she grabbed some scissors, cut the feet out of a pair of control-top pantyhose and slipped them on. That was the beginning.

As we can see, having got an idea, Sara did not stop but began working on bringing it to life. This is how she saw her life mission — to make women's life even more attractive.

At first, she made the prototype of her product at home. Then she went to all lingerie manufacturers in her area to offer them her invention. For this matter, she arranged a meeting with a lawyer to get her idea patented. The lawyer could not believe that the woman in front of him really meant what she was saying. He thought it was a joke and that he was filmed by a hidden camera. Still, he told her that the price for registration of a trademark would be from $3,000 to $5,000. Sara only had $5,000 which she had saved, and she decided not to spend them on registration, but to patent her product on her own. Sara read several books on trademarks and patents wrote the patent herself and later found a lawyer who helped write the claims. After that, she thought about the name by studying the history of names of all well-known companies.

Sara knew that Kodak and Coca-Cola were the two most recognized names in the world, and they both have a predominant "K" sound in them. This sound had something special about it. The name of "Kodak" never existed and was invented by its owner, but still the letter magic worked. Sara invented the name "Spanx" as it met the requirement to have the sound "k" in the name.

Dear reader, can you see Sara thoroughly studying the whole process of registration and assigning a name to her company?

Having registered her patent, she took a week off work and drove around North Carolina to see all the lingerie manufacturers who refused her offer in writing. Now, they refused her offer in a face-to-face meeting. In several days, one of the owners gave her an unexpected positive answer. He explained that his two daughters were amazed by Sara's invention. Now Sarah created a ready-made product and the factory developed the manufacturing process for her invention from A to Z.

Sara did not pay attention to different obstacles and difficulties. She knew what she wanted. She realized her purpose and carried it out boldly. It revealed all her potential and her extraordinary personality.

As a result, Sara could invest all her savings of $5,000 and made some samples of her product. Then she needed a sales market. She visited many lingerie shops and bought samples by all well-known manufacturers. At home, she analyzed the packaging. It was gray and boring. Then she developed the design of her packaging on her own making it bright and colorful. Then she started looking for sales markets. She called every shop and company engaged in selling such products. In one company, she was told that the director could meet her but she would only have 10 minutes of time. In no time, Sara took a plane and went for the presentation in New York. In the first five minutes of the presentation, Sara felt her speech was not too convincing. She took a risk and broke the plan of her presentation; she just asked the woman who was the director to try her invention on. To her surprise, the director agreed, and soon signed an agreement with Sara for supplies of her product.

Now you understand that you have to be passionate and confident of the uniqueness of your idea to hold such an extraordinary presentation. Her courage was rewarded. While she was going to the airport, she called the factory owner and shouted loudly that she had signed the contract and needed a lot of products. The owner was amazed and replied: "I thought you would be selling the 1,000 items we produced until you retired."

An unexpected turn of events, due to the persistence of the inventor, isn't it? It happened — thanks to the person who realized her life mission, revealed herself and confidently went to her goal. The sales began. Sara called all her friends and begged them to visit shops and make a huge fuss over the product and buy it up. This way she managed to organize her sales.

One day, Sara sent her product just as a present to Oprah Winfrey. It was surprising when Oprah called and thanked Sara for her present. She suggested that Sara come on her show and shoot a program about her unique product. The program crew went to Sara's house to film how she works with her team in her office. Sara had to contact her friends to ask them to play along with her, presenting themselves as members of her team. The film crew could not believe that she did all the work herself. After Oprah's show Spanx products became very popular.

THE PERSON WHO KNOWS HIS CALLING WILL FIND OPPORTUNITIES EVERYWHERE

He will not be embarrassed in front of the great and famous people because he knows who he is, and he knows the purpose of his life.

Only after five years of starting her business could Sara afford to hire three people as members of her team. The company office is still in her apartment.

In this way, Sara was able to earn 1 billion dollars and become a leader in the underwear industry by the age of 41.

She went through the process of implementation of her vision from A to Z. She did not have an initial capital and she did not invest a single dollar into advertising. She registered the patent herself, made a stunning packaging of her products and developed the first sample of the goods herself. She displayed her perseverance in finding a manufacturer who created and launched the production of goods. She found sales markets thanks to her unusual presentation, and because of her tremendous persistence, her product has become known throughout the country and around the world. She organized a team of like-minded people and they still work together.

If Sara did it, each of us can do it. You just have to be firm, persistent, passionate, and driven by the idea and have a strong desire to bring your product to the market. Of course, the product must be in demand, necessary and useful for consumers. Sara did it. Now it's up to you!

SPECIFIC STEPS FROM YOUR DREAM TO ITS FULFILLMENT

Set a particular goal

Find out: what kind of goal do you want to achieve?

For example, if I want to make a stew, then how many people should it be for?

You have to set yourself a particular goal: What kind of goal do I really want to achieve?

The time period

How much time do I have?

For example: How much time do I have to make a stew? — A year, a month, a day or an hour?

You have to ask yourself: how much time do I need to implement this goal?

How much time do I have to make a stew? A year, a month or a day?

This is necessary in order to help us plan our actions in time: for a day, a week, a month, a year, etc.

If we do not set the time limits, we can get caught up in the process and never achieve the goal.

Territory

Where do I want to implement my goal?

London or Cambridge?

England or Scotland?

Set up a sports club — where, in what area?

Where do you want to implement your idea, where do you want to set up your business?

Do you want to build a chocolate factory? Where? In what area? Why do you want to build it in this place? Is it in downtown or in the country? What influences your decision?

You have to find out which resources are scarce

Conduct an audit to see what resources you already have. You have at least:

Your head; Eyes; Hands; Knowledge.

You have to find out what other resources you need to achieve your goal.

You have to determine what you can do with the resources already available

People, time, money. At least you already have a head, hands and legs. You are the main resource.

Let us think about Sara again; she coped with her task, having only herself, her life as a resource. We have eyes, body, knowledge, what else do you need? Sara had just an idea and she did not have anything but her dream came true.

What can you do with the resources already available?

How to start?

You have to determine what steps will be first.

Divide the task into time periods

It means to "divide your elephant into small pieces." Divide the big task into small pieces which can be done every day and start working.

The big goal does not frighten you anymore, you can keep it for the future, but there are things which you can do: "What do I need to do in a certain period of time: one month, one week, one day?"

What is a plan?

A plan is not a routine that a man does every day; it is not even a timetable. The plan concerns your life, your calling. You have to write down what you really want to do in this life and then you have to write down what you have to do every day to achieve the goal. You have to write down all your everyday steps.

From the above story, we see that Sara had a steady job that provides her with some income. She also had a dream — the idea of creating female corrective underwear. And her plans concerned her dreams, her real purpose, and not daily routine and work. She took steps to achieve her life goal in her spare time, in her time off.

If during the day, a person did not do anything about his purpose and calling, he did nothing at all.

Every day you need to do something about your purpose of life.

Dividing the goal into pieces must be brought down to the smallest measurable element, a day, to know exactly what to do every day.

For example, you are faced with the task of finding 30 persons per month for the sales of your product; it means that you need to find one person a day. Thus, it is necessary to think how to perform the daily task, not a task for a month. You must take a general goal or task that you have and divide it into stages.

Let's study it in details.

Suppose you want to cook a soup and you have 5 hours left. Then you split the time into portions which you will need to go shopping, to peel vegetables, and to cook them. Or: you need to find 20 clients in a month for the sale of your goods. This means that every day you need to find one client. It is necessary to divide the task by the time that you have.

You don't need to think about the month. You need to plan the day. You need to take your "elephant" and divide it into pieces and eat a slice every day. No need to think, "Oh, what a huge elephant! What a hard task!" This is wrong! Therefore, many people are afraid of the scale of "the elephant," they constantly think about the large size of this problem. No need to think about it, you just need to keep the problem in perspective.

Sara Blakely did not think every day that her goods must enter the global market, she did not think about how much she needs to invest in advertising. She did every day what she could. The rest she kept in perspective. Her own home became her office, and she did not invest anything in the advertising of her product because she advertised it by herself. You need to break a problem into pieces and do what is scheduled for each time slot. You have to do the planned work for a day. That's all. The rest of the time you can go for a walk, do what you want, but the piece that you have to do during the day is something you must do. Then do all the rest! But you have to do something every day for your dream, for your goal.

Mark Twain wrote 1,000 words a day. Stephen King wrote 10 pages of text a day. You must know what you need to do every day to carry out your mission. You wake up on Tuesday morning, already knowing what you will do for your goal. This is very important, because credit of time in your life is limited. Appreciate and value your time — this is the key to success!

Divide the target in proportion to the available resources

It is necessary to find ways of solving the problem at the expense of available resources.

You must learn to see everything around yourself as your resources, your opportunities, and turn them into your weapons to get them working in your favor, in order to achieve your goal.

Sara Blakely took her time to study from the books how to register a patent. Then she used the packaging of goods in the shops to analyze what her own packages should be like. She had sent her product as a gift to Oprah Winfrey, so she was invited to Oprah's show and millions of Americans heard about her product.

Everything around you is your life and your opportunity. It is a liability, which should be turned into an asset to work for you, in your favor.

About resources practically:

- Computer: how can I solve the problem with this resource?
- The people around me: what can I do with the help of my connections?
- If there are no onions to cook a soup, but I have friends I can cook the soup with the help of my neighbors; this is already a resource, too.

I want to show you on a very simple example that knowledge will help you to solve any problem.

- You do not know how to cook a soup, but there is the Internet, where you can find recipes. So you can solve the problem.

The next step: you need to divide a general problem into parts, and to divide it into available resources, such as people. How can you solve the issue with them and with their help?

Let's say you have a resource of connections. How many problems can you solve with the help of your acquaintances?

Sara used her resources — acquaintances, friends, i.e. people, and with their help, she found the director of a shopping chain selling women's underwear and did an excellent presentation of her goods. This presentation was the beginning of her stunning success. Does it seem to be a coincidence? No, it was all about resources used properly!

Create a Team

It means to find like-minded people, or create a team by yourself.

Sara Blakely created her team in an original way. The first one on her team was her boyfriend, who, seeing how much time her idea took helped her on a voluntary basis. Then, she discussed advantages of Spanx with her friend for half an hour. As a result, Sara invited her to become her PR director. Don't think about the team immediately. As you move on, the key supporters will come.

Divide the task into parts for each team member

Give them the responsibility and the majority, clearly writing out their plans and explain what you are expecting of them. You cannot do everything by yourself. You need to learn how to delegate responsibility and trust people that everything will be done on time and with the highest quality.

The control system

Establish your system of control to see how everyone does his job. The human factor is very important. It is essential to check the quality of work carried out or people may let you down.

Establish a system of rewards and punishments

If it is necessary, you need to set a system of rewards and punishments for yourself and your people.

So these were practical steps on how to start implementation of your dream.

Now the only thing needed is your actions!

CONCLUSIONS

1. Recognition lies in our natural desires.

2. The largest uniqueness of yours is where you are special and differ from others.

3. Things that you love or hate very much can be your destination.

4. It is known that the environment accounts for 50 percent of your success. If you want to become a journalist, you need to communicate with journalists who are professionals in this business. If you see yourself as an outstanding sales manager, you need to find a corresponding environment and attend sales training.

5. Often, we only dream of something, but do not fulfill our purpose, and that's because we do not know how to go from a dream to its fulfillment.

6. People cite two reasons in their defense:
   - I do not know how — a question of the process. You do not understand the process of achieving and fulfilling your dreams.
   - No opportunities: no money, no resources. Both are important to carry out your goals.

7. The most important thing you need to do to accomplish your purpose is to stop, get comfortable, sit down and find time for thinking.

8. You need to study, to examine deeply the field you are interested in. It is necessary to approach the study of

the issue from all sides to find as much information as possible on this issue.

9. It is necessary to build a system or a structure which will allow you to transform your dream into reality.

10. It is necessary to draw up a plan concerning your goals, your calling: it is necessary to write out in details what you need to do every day in regard to your purpose and mission in life.

11. If during the day you did not do anything about your purpose and calling — you did nothing at all.

12. The goal must be divided into a smallest measurable and visible period of time — a day, so you know exactly what to do every day.

13. You do not need to think about a month. You need to plan the day. You need to take your "elephant" and divide it into pieces. Every day you "eat" a slice of it. No need to think, "Oh, what a huge elephant!"

14. You must learn to see everything around yourself as your resources, your opportunities and turn them into your weapons so that everything works in your favor and helps to achieve your goal.

Dear reader, if you have answered all the questions that have been listed above, and have decided on your dream, things you love, your destination, the most important thing for you is to never stop at this stage.

You need to take some time off and delve into the study of the topic you are interested in. You need to do research, to approach the study of the issue from all sides. Find as much information about your subject as you can.

Then, without postponing anything, build a structure that will allow you to transform this vision into reality.

To do it: Make a plan that concerns your purpose, your calling and describes exactly what should be done every day for your purpose and mission of life.

Remember! If during the day a person didn't do anything concerning his purpose and calling, he did nothing at all.

The dividing of purpose into pieces must be brought down to the least measurable and smallest segment — a day, to know exactly what to do every day.

One of the most important things is that you need to write down your goals and plans. It is proved that those who have plans but do not record them, lose to those who have written plans. To fail to plan is to plan to fail.

"If you fail to plan, you plan to fail." (KRIS VALLOTTON)

From 1979 to 1989, Harvard University held a special experiment. Graduates were asked the question: "Have you set yourselves clearly written goals for your future? Have you created any plans to achieve these goals?" The results showed that:

- 3% of the participants had such goals and plans;
- 13% had goals, but did not write them;
- About 84% of the students had no specific purpose, other than to graduate and enjoy the summer fun.

The graduates of this course were interviewed again 10 years later, in 1989. It turned out that the 13% of graduates who had a goal, but didn't write it, earned on average twice more than those 84% of the graduates who didn't set any goals. But the most amazing thing was that the 3% of students, who recorded their goals on paper, earned on average ten times more than the remaining 97% of the graduates combined. The only difference between the three categories was the clarity of their goal-setting.

But the experiment was not over! The researchers found that those 3% of the graduates were also much more successful in their personal and family life. They felt happier, more satisfied, divorces were rare and they were less depressed than the other 97%.

84% are the people who don't have a clear plan in their life; they become the labor force, small elements in the global system of the world.

13% are also small elements of the system because they had a goal in mind, but they did not write it, and they didn't have a clear plan to achieve this goal, so it was impossible to achieve it. They lack the system of achieving their dream through good planning.

So write down your goals, make a plan on paper and follow it strictly.

PART 3

WHAT PREVENTS US FROM FULFILLING OUR CALLING?

Dear reader! In the second part of our book, we have answered the question: "How to find oneself?" We have analyzed the principles of turning a dream into reality, and how to get from A to Z. We have examined the steps of practical implementation, and specific steps from a dream to its realization.

In the third part of the book, we will answer the question: "What prevents us from fulfilling our calling?"

Why do we often fail to achieve our goals? What prevents us from fulfilling our calling?

Why do some people fulfill their dreams without having special talents and gifts, while others, being even more gifted, do not achieve their goal?

CHAPTER 10

WHAT IS AN INFERIORITY COMPLEX AND WHAT CAUSES IT?

WHAT IS AN INFERIORITY COMPLEX AND WHAT CAUSES IT?

Let me tell you about an interesting experiment conducted during the advertising of cosmetic products. A woman was led up to the mirror and asked to assess her appearance. Her words and self-assessment were recorded on a Dictaphone. Then an artist painted a portrait of this woman. The next group of people who were also participants in the experiment looked at the portrait of the woman when it had already been painted by the artist and had to assess her appearance. All stages of the process were filmed. Then the video in which participants assessed the appearance of the women was shown to these women.

The part where women first see the difference between how they described their appearance in words and how other people did it is certainly very touching.

Women do not give a very favorable estimate of their appearance. They are too critical of themselves. But those who saw their portraits painted by the artist liked their appearance very much.

Of course, every woman needs to appreciate her natural beauty, but she also needs to analyze the topic of complexes in general. After all, it is complexes that prevent women with a good appearance from adequately assessing themselves.

This experiment raises an issue of complexes. The topic is not new, but the interesting thing here is that the reality of women was distorted. Women with beautiful appearance could not objectively assess themselves. That's what an inferiority complex does. It distorts reality. When we assess ourselves wrongly, we are mistaken about our abilities; the result is that we cannot see our ability to achieve a goal. So a complex, by distorting our perception of ourselves in our mind, builds obstacles that prevent achievement of our goals.

A complex is stealing energy from our personality and we constantly worry about the fact that we are not the most intelligent and successful ones. We fear that we are ugly, that we cannot succeed, and we are afraid of something. And the energy that is necessary for us to achieve the goal is spent on meaningless anxiety. As a result, we will not achieve our goals. We are afraid; we are not confident; we are indecisive; and to a greater extent, we are passive. What is this complex and what causes it?

Different teachers give us different answers to this question, but if you try to find something in common in their definitions, then most likely it will sound like "something that distorts our perception of ourselves and the world."

So the first step in getting rid of complexes — and, consequently, to finding a more conscious and harmonious life — is to see and understand where these distortions occur in our lives.

The more distortions we have, the less attention we can pay to realizing our potential and self-actualization of our personalities.

Imagine that every day you get 100% of the energy and you can invest it either in self-realization and the achievement of your goals or in the struggle with yourself or the world around you. You can spend the energy received to achieve goals, implement plans for self-education, sport, and healthy lifestyle. That is, you use the received energy to gain self-actualization. But for many people, a huge part of the energy goes into the struggle with complexes, fears, worries, anxieties, and the energy cannot be used to achieve goals and dreams, which, in turn, leads to cases of unrealized potential.

As Robin Sharma says, *"unrealized potential turns into pain,"* which means an even bigger set of complexes.

How much of your daily energy is spent on dissatisfaction and irritation about the people around you?

Estimate what percentage of the energy that is gained every day goes to the denial of yourself and others, on the negative mood, negative internal dialogues, self-criticism, dissatisfaction, comparing yourself to others, fear, rejection, and self-pity? To reduce this percentage, it is necessary to understand the most important reason which prevents us from feeling like a happy person on the way to self-actualization.

This is the inferiority complex. The larger the complex, the more energy it takes away from us. The more energy taken, the less energy that is left for us to implement our plans and goals, and the smaller the probability of realization of our innate potential.

> *"If something drives me forward, then it is my weakness, which I hate and therefore turn into my strength."* (MICHAEL JEFFREY JORDAN, ALL AMERICAN BASKETBALL PROFESSIONAL)

Many people are confused by their own behavior. They do not understand why they cannot do well in their lives, even with a lot of training, using short-term and long-term plans, and, most importantly, having a huge potential.

Everyone should think about why certain undesirable situations occur in life. Why is a person with a great gift or talent unable to fulfill his destination in life? What is the main obstacle to the success of our self-actualization? Successful self-actualization can prevent inferiority complexes. An Inferiority complex is acquired in childhood. It is known that human thinking is formed in the first five to seven years. What is the influence of the environment on the formation of the child's thinking and, subsequently, on his future life?

Both positive and negative thinking can be formed in a child. Negative thinking is based on complexes. Psychological structure of the complex remains with the person for life, having been formed in early childhood. Alfred Adler believes that an inferiority complex is universal, common to all people, and the only question is how it is compensated in a socially useful, reasonable, or useless way.

The works by famous psychologists Antonio Megetti and Erich Fromm state that an inferiority complex is formed during the first years of life because of the nature of love that a child receives. (Erich Fromm. "Escape from Freedom". AST, Moscow, 2009. P.3–40, Alfred Adler. Analytical psychology // History of foreign psychology: Texts. M., 1986, P. 131–142).

If a child is loved, he feels worthy of love in the future. If he is roughly treated and not respected and not shown love, the child will have problems with self-esteem.

The child accepts role models of parental behavior unconsciously and, without thinking, he will take it that he is not worthy of love if parents don't give him love, because they are the highest authority for him. For example, if a child is constantly criticized in the family, he ceases to dream and develops a negative attitude toward himself, and does not believe in his own strength. In adult life, he will be deprived of energy, enthusiasm, and he will be critical of himself.

A child is not to blame for being immersed in a certain environment and handed down complexes. For parents, it is important to respect the personality of a child.

In order to change thinking into the positive way, we need to analyze what complexes we have received. When a complex is acquired, personal development is stopped, and the person even being an adult, sometimes behaves in a childish and immature way.

Dr. Wilder Penfield, director of the Montreal Neurological Institute, conducted experiments that showed:

- The cortex contains a kind of an endless cinematic film, depicting everything that we have experienced in reality since childhood.

- Our brain functions like a high-quality computer.

- Feelings associated with past experiences are also recorded in close connection with them.

- Personality can exist in two states. The patient knew that he was on the operating table and talked to Penfield (his doctor). But he also knew that he had seen "the building of Seven-Up" and "Harrison's bakery" (his childhood). He was in two planes. At the same time — in the experience (the recollection of his childhood), feeling it, and also outside of it (on the operating table), watching it.

- The recorded experiences and feelings associated with them are available for replay today in the same living form, as at their first appearance, and determine the nature of today's behavior. Experience can not only be remembered but also revived. The patient did not only remember what he felt. He experienced this feeling again in the present time.

As you can see, complexes and negative beliefs remain in our subconsciousness for a lifetime. Our subconscious mind stores all our negative beliefs, complexes, and behavioral patterns. The main strength of the subconscious mind is that it stores ALL OF A PERSON'S BELIEFS.

All that it considers true and undoubted will sooner or later get into the subconsciousness. It takes root there, creating an overall picture of the world. We need to analyze our picture of the world. It is necessary to analyze all the restricting beliefs and complexes, which we acquired in childhood, from the family, school and society. And then we should get rid of these restricting attitudes and systems of belief in order to remove obstacles in our way to the achievement of our goals and revealing our potential.

If a person who grew up in an unhappy family cannot reprogram the subconsciousness he will not be able to create a strong marital union in the future. This is because his subconsciousness keeps the memory of past conflicts, quarrels and other negative occurrences in the family, which continue to affect the person and determine his actions in the present.

As a result, your subconscious mind will do its best to keep you from a successful marriage, because you have a disagreement between your consciousness and subconsciousness. For example, you aspire to marriage but your subconsciousness struggles to protect you and take away the threat of marriage because in the subconscious mind you have a mindset that marriage is a negative event that leads you to a catastrophe.

Subconsciousness is extremely selfish, it will do anything to keep you safe and remain in a comfort zone.

Negative beliefs and complexes are stored in your subconscious mind and create a weakness, which will not let you succeed in life. They will be an obstacle to success and achievement and fulfilling goals. When a child is immersed in a certain environment, his thinking is formed by role models of behavior demonstrated by parents in the family who have had a great influence on the formation of thinking of the child. These mindsets or complexes can be feelings of guilt, a victim complex, and fear of failure, criticism, poverty, and loneliness, loss of love, success, insecurity, denial, and low self-esteem.

CHAPTER 11

FEELINGS OF GUILT

FEELINGS OF GUILT

Helen grew up in a family where the relationship between parents left much to be desired. The father was strict and tough; he was rarely at home, and always engaged in his business. He had a cold attitude to his daughter — as well as to his wife. The mother was always criticizing and reproaching Helen. If the girl did something wrong, there was a loud reprimand with blame and shame as the focus. The father never showed attention or affection to Helen. The girl grew up in the atmosphere of indifference and constant rows. As a result, Helen did not think she was worthy of love because the people who were supposed to love her did not respect her and never accepted her or showed their affection to her.

When she was 14, she kept to a diet and lost 15lbs; she hardly ate anything and monitored her weight scrupulously because she only could accept herself if she complied with fashion model standards. Her mother was at a loss because Helen stopped eating healthy food, developed a stomach disease but refused to be examined by a doctor or to admit that she does really strange things. Her mother felt it was not just a diet and there was something else to follow. Soon Helen developed a complex concerning her appearance. Thinking about her looks being far from perfect led her to serious depression.

What do you think? Can a person in such a state achieve his goal or search for his destination? Certainly, he cannot. All of Helen's energy was spent on meaningless worries, let alone life goals and answering the question "Who am I?" As a result,

Helen applied to medics for therapy and psychological help. Her actions were based on wrong mindsets planted into her subconsciousness in her childhood. Because of Helen's lack of love and attention in her childhood, she developed an idea that she could be accepted and loved only with a fashion model appearance. She began experimenting with diets and did all kinds of possible and impossible things to comply with globally accepted standards. Then her complex known as feelings of guilt or self-rejection went off. Helen required a long course of therapy to accept herself the way she is and believe that she deserves love even if her appearance is far from perfect.

In the first place, she needed to understand that she is not her appearance or her body. She is the characteristics, values and beliefs that are inherent only to her. This is her uniqueness and her peculiarity. She can be loved and accepted even if her weight does not meet global standards. Helen understood that she is not only a beautiful body but a unique personality.

In the second place, she had to reveal herself to the destination and the goal of life. After Helen accepted herself, she found the answer to the question of her destination.

The complex known as feelings of guilt does not let us accept ourselves the way we are created. We do not see our uniqueness. Without accepting it, we try to meet requirements of society and do everything to be accepted. We don't ask ourselves the question "Who am I?" and don't think about the sense of life and our life mission. All energy given to us to achieve the goal and self-actualization is directed towards being accepted by our surroundings, to meet their requirements. As a result, our goals are still not achieved.

Helen worked on herself, her thinking and self-esteem. This work helped her to conquer the negative complex. She changed her attitude to herself and her appearance. She graduated from a university, had a job she likes, she is married and now lives in another city, apart from her parents and in pursuit of a successful career. She is happy in her marriage, engaged in self-actualization and full of faith and optimism. Helen's unwillingness to accept herself prevented her self-actualization and search of answers to the questions "Who am I?" and "Where am I going?"

WHAT DOES THIS PATTERN OF BEHAVIOR OR GUILT COMPLEX LOOK LIKE?

A child is scolded for breaking an expensive vase but he is not guilty. He cannot control his movements properly yet, and we, as adults, have to keep expensive things away from children. The child learns to be guilty when he is punished and scolded for damaging material objects. Parents are labeling, criticizing and reproaching the child on any account. "What good can become of you? Stupid, failure, dumb-head." Later on, constant criticism makes the person accustomed to a negative attitude towards himself and therefore he feels no love for himself, cannot accept himself, and thinks in a negative way: I am a loser, I am dumb, I am ignorant, I am ugly.

The feelings of guilt take away self-confidence, reduces self-esteem, welcomes fears, confusion, disappointment, despondency, pessimism and depression. Guilt takes away the energy and strength and reduces a person's productivity.

A man is constantly engaged in a dialogue with himself during which he accuses himself, expresses dissatisfaction with himself and his actions. Accidents and illnesses are accepted as deserved retribution by the person who has feelings of guilt. He can also believe that he deserves a critical attitude towards himself, and accidents and illnesses come as a punishment for his incorrect behavior. His mind contains a negative way of thinking, he criticizes himself, and he has no respect for himself and therefore allows the people around him to treat him accordingly. He believes that he does not deserve better treatment. This complex prevents a person from being a fully valued personality. Certainly, a person with such a complex finds it hard to implement his potential because he is hampered by a distorted vision of himself.

WHAT IS THE DANGER OF THIS COMPLEX?

Recently, there was much publicity about the book by Dr. Masaru Emoto "Messages of Water." It featured unique photographs of ice crystals formed out of the water subjected to various non-physical influences. At first, Dr. Emoto influenced the crystallizing water with music, ranging from Beethoven to heavy metal bands, and photographed the results. Having justified that music has an undisputed influence on the size and shape of crystals, he also tested the influence of consciousness on the water. After all, music is quite a material physical phenomenon (a set of sound waves) that can influence matter. What about emotions? Dr. Emoto placed labels with various human ideas and emotions written on them onto tubes of water. Some labels had positive ideas, such as "Thank you" or "Love" while others had negative information on them, e.g. "You make me sick" or "I will kill you!" Contrary to beliefs generally accepted by modern science, the water reacted to the inscriptions despite the fact that these words did not interact with the water directly. Water in tubes with positive inscriptions froze into beautiful and regularly shaped crystals. The water in tubes with negative inscriptions turned into ugly and shapeless crystals. If thoughts can do such things to water, you can only imagine what thoughts can do to us!

We contain 60% water, so what can our thoughts do to us? Negative thoughts about us and our life may deprive us of our health.

We underestimate ourselves, we do not believe in our strength, abilities, and talents and we have a distorted vision of ourselves. Because of that, we do not believe that we can reach the goal or fulfill our destination, though we feel we have the necessary potential.

Negative thoughts about ourselves steal our energy. We dedicate most of the time worrying about our deficiencies and self-criticism. As a result, we fail to concentrate on our goals and cannot believe in our destination. Sometimes we are so upset about our meaningless worries that we keep losing focus of the goal all the time. We can reach the goal but it is going to take an incredible amount of time and effort.

HOW TO GET RID OF THE FEELING OF GUILT?

Files of the past can be changed through shock, encouragement or pain.

Life can be spent in an atmosphere of continuous encouragement, you will ignore the complex and it will disappear.

Another way is pain — you cannot act in the old way, as you got used to, as you have been programmed in your childhood, and you will have to change yourself otherwise you will not survive.

Affirmations — thinking can be changed through the pronunciation of the Word of God in your life, because it contains enough strength and energy to change your subconsciousness. For example, "I accept myself the way I am,

I accept God's love for me, my creation is a wonder."

Creation of a new habit. For example, you are indecisive, but if you start practicing all the time, making decisions quickly and act in accordance with your decisions, you will be able to acquire a new habit.

THE GOLDEN NUGGETS

1. The complex called the feeling of guilt does not let us accept ourselves the way we are created. We do not see our uniqueness.

2. Without accepting ourselves, we try to meet requirements of society and do everything to be accepted. We do not ask the question "Who am I?" and do not think about the sense of life and our life mission. All energy given to us for the achievement of goals and self-actualization is instead spent on deriving acceptance from our surroundings and on compliance with the requirements of society. As a result, our goals are never achieved.

SELF-EXAMINATION TEST

1. **Do you often criticize yourself?**
   a) Yes, I do it often (0)
   b) I often criticize myself but I realize that criticism does not help me to achieve my goals so I am working to change my thoughts about myself (1)
   c) I only accept sound criticism, and I do not indulge in self-criticism (2)

2. **What is your attitude to compliments?**
   a) I am embarrassed (0)
   b) Sometimes it is difficult to accept them (1)
   c) I take praise calmly if it is not about flattery (2)

3. **Can you apply a negative epithet to yourself, in your thoughts, apply a negative evaluation of yourself?**
   a) Yes, I do it often (0)
   b) Yes, I sometimes think about myself that way (1)
   c) Never, I respect myself (2)

4. **Do you compare yourself to others?**
   b) Yes, and it's not in my favor (0)
   c) I try to combat this habit but I do not always succeed (1)
   d) I have no time for that (2)

5. **Do you happen to be disappointed in you or your actions?**
   a) Yes, and quite often (0)
   b) It happens sometimes but I am trying to struggle against this habit (1)
   c) No, something may go wrong, but I never feel disappointed in my personality (2)

Test Results

0–4 points — We are sorry, but you do not accept yourself, underestimate your potential and indulge in self-criticism. With such way of thinking, it is very difficult for you to achieve your goals and fulfill your destination. Your thinking steals too much energy and time. We advise that you should apply practical tasks of this chapter and we hope for your victory over yourself.

5–9 points — Sometimes you feel the influence of this complex and you can distinguish when negative self-criticism and low self-esteem appear, and you work on your way of thinking. You have to put an end to the complex because such thinking leads you to defeat and makes it much harder for you to accomplish your goals. Keep on working and the victory will be yours!

9–12 points — We are glad for you! You are not prone to the feeling of guilt, you have an adequate self-esteem, and all your energy is spent on achieving the goals you have set so you are most effective in achieving your objective.

PRACTICAL TASKS

1. **If you discovered having this complex you need to change the way of thinking.** In order to do so, compose affirmations that change your thinking.

2. **Affirmations should be pronounced during 21 days to change your thoughts about yourself, e.g.** "I accept myself the way I am; I am created to be a unique personality etc."

3. **Go through new patterns of behavior in your consciousness during 21days to constantly have the picture of what you would like to be.**

Recommended reading

||||||||||||||||||||||||||||||||||||||||||||||||||||||||||||||||||||||||||||||

For a more detailed study of the topic I recommend reading the books "Freedom from fear" and "My ego and I. Who wins?"

CHAPTER 12

VICTIM MENTALITY

VICTIM MENTALITY

Emma grew up in a matriarchal-dominated family. She had a tough and imperious mother, and a gentle and weak-willed drunkard father. Her mother dominated everyone else and decided on everyone's life including her husband, Emma and her brother. When the time to choose a good university for Emma's education came, it was not even mentioned that Emma could choose it on her own. Emma did not learn to take responsibility in dealing with problems; she was accustomed to the fact that her mother made all the decisions concerning her life.

She was incapable of building her life independently. Moreover, Emma pitied herself when her mother treated her in an unjust way, as she saw it. All these emotional experiences and regrets became her life companions. She exhibited a sense of dissatisfaction because of realizing her inner potential and being unable to see her life fulfilled. Emma was unable to think, come to conclusions, analyze people's behavior on her own and work on the eradication of her weaknesses. She preferred to live justifying her conduct. As a result, she remained an example of victim mentality and this complex prevented her from self-actualization.

A man with a victim mentality attracts autocrats into his life who will decide how he should live. How can a person with such mentality find himself, his life mission and go towards his aim? Such people consider actions such as making decisions, setting goals and achieving them to be nothing more than formidable obstacles. It is easier to be a mere performer and not to make serious decisions, to live with an assistance of someone else's mind and obey someone's commands for people with this type of character. They do not have a habit of thinking on their own or thinking in general.

A man with a victim mentality feels like being a victim who is complaining and crying all the time. Constant complaints created more situations where Emma was forced to play the role of victim. She has never learned how to build relations on a mutually beneficial ground. It was very difficult for her to say "no" and she did others' work beyond all reasonable boundaries. She felt being used by someone, though she agreed to work on her own free will. At long last, all relationships ended in a mental strain, rows and accusation of employers, friends, and colleagues without reflecting on the core of the problem. Everything ended with accusations and complaints.

This is the main problem of a person with a victim mentality. He is incapable of thinking over his life and, consequently, cannot reach his goals effectively. People with such mentality often do not have any life purpose, because they do not know how to acquire them unless someone plans their future for them. Victims always complain and object to something. They spend their energy not on achieving their target but on meaningless complaints. A person with this complex gets accustomed to life with an assistance of someone's mind, waiting for someone to make decisions for him, he is unable to make decisions by himself and he is always in need of advice and prompts. A human being should learn to make decisions independently in order to achieve goals efficiently.

As a result, Emma who is 40 now has not learned how to build her life on her own, and she waits for advice from her friends and attracts situations where she appears as a victim.

Despite her potential, it is very difficult for her to be realized in life and achieve goals effectively.

As a rule, children of tough and imperious parents sticking to authoritarian methods of upbringing have a victim complex. Children get used to the thought that their fate depends on powerful parents deciding everything in their life. They consider life to be beyond their power in the same way as a child expects someone to decide his fate.

A child is treated badly, his point of view is not respected, and he is not a person who is ever taken into account. A child gets used to being insignificant and formulates a conclusion that he is a victim.

A person with a victim complex is afraid of hearing the word "no" and being refused. It means to be an outcast. That is why such a person is afraid of asking for something, he is afraid of being refused.

Having a conversation with somebody, a person with a victim complex starts to complain of people who destroyed his life, or lack of means of subsistence, or of poor health. Other people lose all desire to keep on communicating with this person. A "victim" is narrow-minded. For example, he has such an approach towards life problems: "I cannot afford it", but "I must". For instance, sitting at the desk on a Friday evening the "victim" will be thinking despondently: "I must finish this work as soon as possible, but I cannot complete it within such a small period of time. Consequently, I should take it home one more time."

The manager at the next desk will be doing the same amount of work trying to concentrate on it and direct all energy to achieve the set goals. He is not interrupted by meaningless mental strains and he is more effective merely on this account.

He will complete it sooner and will not take it home. The negative way of thinking based on constant complaints, strains and objections of discontent steals our energy. As a result, a person works slower and is inclined to take his work home.

WHY IS THE VICTIM COMPLEX SO DANGEROUS?

1. People susceptible to it are accustomed to having all decisions being made by their parents and later by their spouses, employers, or friends instead of making decisions and fulfilling them by themselves.

2. They automatically attract imperious and authoritative individuals in their lives.

3. They find it impossible to depend upon themselves to solve in dealing with problems and tend to wait for a savior.

4. They attract people in their lives that tease them, abuse them and even bully them instead of building mutually beneficial relationships.

HOW TO CHANGE IF YOU HAVE A VICTIM COMPLEX

1. Get rid of the old stereotype "I am a victim."

2. Start making decisions on your own and live using your own mind.

3. Take responsibility for your life and count solely on yourself.

4. Identify the purpose of your life and its destination and work out a plan to achieve your goal.

5. Step beyond the scopes and limits, because a narrow-minded person has such boundaries of thinking "I cannot, but I must".

6. Get to know how to rely on yourself and think independently and never wait for a savior.

So, give up negative thinking and realize your potential. Answer the questions "Who am I? Where am I going?" Work out a plan of achieving your goal and go forward to achievements and fulfillments.

CONCLUSIONS

1. As we can see, first of all, this complex creates obstacles in the way of our identification it prevents us from making it by ourselves without a friend's, a husband's, a wife's or parent's help. You must answer the question "Who am I?" on your own.

2. A person with a victim complex is incapable of achieving his goal without someone's assistance, advice and prompts.

3. A person with a victim complex loses energy on constant complaints and objections.

4. A person with a victim complex is unable to set goals and achieve them independently.

THE GOLDEN NUGGETS

1. People having a victim complex cannot make decisions themselves. They expect their parents, later — spouses, employers or friends to decide everything for them.

2. People having victimhood attract imperious and authoritative individuals in their life.

3. People having a victim complex are not apt to count on themselves in dealing with problems and they tend to wait for a savior.

4. People having a victim complex invite someone to tease them into their lives though they could have mutually beneficial relationships.

5. People with a victim complex are incapable of reaching their goals without someone's assistance, advice and prompts.

6. People with a victim complex lose energy on constant complaints and objections, and they cannot reach their life goals.

7. People with a victim complex are unable to set goals and achieve them.

SELF-EXAMINATION TEST

1. **Do you have any difficulties in making decisions on your own?**
   a) I virtually do not make decisions independently. I need advice and prompts (0)
   b) I work on making decisions by my own (1)
   c) I easily make decisions and fulfill them (2)

2. **Do you often complain of life and injustice?**
   a) Yes, because people treat me in an unfair way very frequently (0)
   b) Yes, I complain of injustice but try to restrict myself in doing this (1)
   c) Anything can be completed with complaints, so I do not waste time on them (2)

3. **Do you need someone's assistance when having a crisis in your life?**
   a) Definitely, I have difficulties in dealing with obstacles without external help (0)
   b) I work on dealing with problems without external help (1)
   c) I do not need any external help in overcoming obstacles (2)

4. **Do you often meet people who manipulate your personality and make decisions instead of you?**
   a) I am surrounded by such people (0)
   b) Yes, but I try to interact with them at mutually beneficial conditions (1)
   c) I rule my life by myself (2)

TEST RESULTS

0–4 scores — We regret but you have such a complex. You have a lot of difficulties in making decisions yourself; you need a piece of advice or prompt. You cannot reach your goal because of constant objections of discontent, complaints, and all these things steal your energy that should have been directed to solving problems. You are not accustomed to thinking on your own. It is a complex task to set goals and achieve them and fulfill your life destination with such a mentality.

5–9 scores — Sometimes you feel the impact of this complex. You can have a desire to complain of the injustice of the entire world but you struggle with it. You learn to make decisions on your own and to set goals. So, you are on the way to success.

9–12 scores — We are happy for you! You are not vulnerable to this negative complex and you direct all your all energy to achieve your goals.

PRACTICAL TASKS

During 21 days, try to make independent decisions on your own, do it quickly even when they turn out to be incorrect later. They should not be globally important decisions: they can be connected with a choice of food or things to buy etc. Make yourself obey a rule that you should not spend more than 5 seconds on making such decisions.

Recommended reading

I advise you to read the book "What is wrong with me?" by "The University of Life" in order to study this topic better.

CHAPTER 13

THE FEAR OF FAILURE

THE FEAR OF
FAILURE

Why is fear considered to be a negative complex?

There are two forms of fear: a natural fear that is meant for protection and an acquired fear.

We are going to focus on two major fears that hinder successful realization of our potential: fear of failure and fear of criticism or refusal.

We feel a fear of failure in childhood when we are punished for doing something new and unknown. We are reprimanded and punished for trying to accomplish these attempts: "Stop doing it, why did you do it?"

Fear of failure is one of the principal fears creating obstacles in the way of successful self-actualization and achieving goals. This fear is closely connected with the apprehension of failure in any field of life, such as career, business, education or private life.

> "A thought that the efforts taken will not lead to any results dominates a personality and forces to give up even the slightest attempts," (CLAIMED DAVID BURNS, AN AMERICAN PSYCHOTHERAPIST)

Accordingly, to research works conducted by a well-known psychologist, and a Professor of Harvard University, David McCelland states, fear *"of failure is expressed in indecisiveness, incorrect goal-setting and a striving to be no worse than others"*.

People with a distinctly displayed fear of failure are prone to do their work well and with good coordination only in cases when their tasks require simple skills. However, when they encounter more complicated tasks of a problem nature, the quality of work becomes worse, while it improves in cases of people with motivation for success. Fear of failure is expressed in negative goal-setting, indecisiveness, and fear of adverse consequences.

You will have a lot of difficulties in achieving goals if you are indecisive and if you are afraid of incorrect actions. This complex steals our energy with the help of misgivings, strains, and fear of consequences for wrong decisions. We feel it is better not to make an attempt — i.e. not to try to attain the set goals than to go belly up.

Fear of failure impedes adequate self-identification because we would understand that fear is not a special feature of the human being, if we saw ourselves from the Creator's point of view. We were created fearless in order to achieve our goals more effectively.

The main reason for fear of failure lies in people's being unaware of the impact of misfortune on achieving success. The rule is this: you have to lose in order to win. Misfortune is nothing more than a presupposition of success. The greatest success can be the greatest failure very frequently. Success is a game of big numbers. There is a direct link between the quantity of attempts made and the probability of successful result.

HOW DOES FEAR OF FAILURE MANIFEST ITSELF?

A person has an image of uncertain thoughts in his mind that make him smaller, restrict him and do not let him live using the best of his possibilities and reveal his potential; they make him live without passion and cause his life to be gray and filled with daily routine.

This way of thinking distorts our truly self-perception and prevents us from fulfilling our destination. It steals our energy that should be released for achieving our goals.

The main reason for the suppressing feeling of fear is low self-esteem. We estimate ourselves to be worse than we really are. This powerful form of lack of confidence creates a system of thinking that restricts us in order to stop our attempts at advancement and improvement of our life and achieving new aims. This is a distortion of our soul and identification in itself.

Those who operate from a base of fear of failure often procrastinate in making decisions. They do not realize that they just moved away from a happy fulfilling life because of it. Successful people are not afraid of putting everything at stake; they make decisions every single minute.

A decision arouses energy in us and gives us new power. When making a decision, we are connected to the reserve of hidden energy that we have. Choosing something with the help of your sound mind or coming to conclusions ignites a stream of power and energy. Your brain sends an alarm for all the body to stand up and start to act in the direction of this decision. Your brain inspires all your body to fulfill it.

Those who fear failure miss all of that. They are afraid of making decisions and do not have enough resolution and are not inclined to live where they are assigned to live only on this account. Their superfluous prudence prevents them from attaining success and being quick to act.

So, fear of failure steals our energy that we should use to achieve our goals. It distorts our true being and we are mistaken while answering the question: "Who am I?"

Fear of failure does not allow us to make decisions when problems occur, we are not active enough and that is why our opportunities escape us.

We lose our energy provided by the organism meant to help us to achieve our goals because of strains and fear of failure. And certainly, we cannot achieve our goals because of it.

HOW TO GET RID OF THE FEAR OF FAILURE?

1. Meeting fear face-to-face causes it to grow weaker and smaller. It loses control of your emotions. However, if you yield under its pressure, it will spread out and control your feelings and thoughts.

2. You should make your fear into small pieces. For example, we are afraid of being outcast and deprived of people's support and label this feeling a fear of criticism. Our advancement towards our purpose and desire to achieve it are more powerful than the fear of criticism. We overcome it in such a way. Each of us is capable of conquering our fear and we must do it. There are some extra methods of overcoming your fear.

3. You should always be engaged in increasing the level of your self-esteem. This method is based on a principle that people, having higher self-esteem, are capable of coping with fears easier. The interesting thing is that it does not matter whether the self-esteem is adequate or not.

4. Faith. Faith in a supreme power, God, a guardian angel, the Universe makes us feel protected from fears. Believing in a God who knows your name and looks after you helps you to remain standing in combat with fear.

5. Love. Perhaps everyone knows situations when mothers accomplished incredible things by saving their children's lives and men overcame their most terrifying fears for the sake of the women they loved.

It is essential to remember that all positive emotions help a man to conquer fear, and negative thoughts only reduce one's bravery.

In spite of using a phrase "to combat fear" above, it is not completely right. A human being cannot struggle against fear because it is an unequal struggle. Fear is fed by the energy of struggle and becomes invincible. Do not dodge it; confess it to yourself that you are afraid of it. You will obtain more strength after doing it, and your fear will become weaker.

Confessing the existence of fear is not meant to show your weakness, and bravery is not a negation of fear, but ability to act in defiance of your fear. Having started to overcome it, you get through negative emotions. It means that you let fear take away your strength. Admit that you are afraid of your fear and switch your attention over to something else. For fear, ignoring it means the destruction of it.

CHAPTER 14

FEAR OF CRITICISM

FEAR OF CRITICISM

Fear of criticism is a fear of refusal, a fear of being criticized. This is the second reason why people do not set goals. Since childhood, our dreams and hopes suffer blows from criticism and mockery of others. It is possible that our parents did not want us to cherish our highest dreams and then be disappointed, therefore they quickly pointed out to us the reasons why we cannot achieve our goals. Fear of criticism and public opinions strongly oppress every person that it is scientifically proven that emaciation and exhaustion do not come from physical fatigue, but from us trying to accomplish the following, from morning till night:

- to please everyone
- to look well
- to behave correctly
- to adjust to the public opinion.

This creates a constant state of being strained, and as a consequence what you get is stress and exhaustion. Just think how much of your efforts you spend to adjust to other people?

Because of this complex, because of being afraid that our activities, our business, our product may be criticized, we stop and never achieve goals. Fear of criticism steals the energy that we need to direct to the achievement of our goals. If we are criticized, we start to get upset and underestimate ourselves, rather than fix those things for which we are criticized. Fear of criticism distorts proper perception of ourselves and leads us to low self-esteem. We find it difficult to correctly answer the question "Who am I?" because we do not see the advantages in us, and we often compare ourselves to others — not in our favor.

To accept criticism, you need to have the power. "Criticism is a poison for the weak and a medicine for the strong."

Our enemies and friends laughed at us when we imagined ourselves to be someone or did something that exceeded their perceptions of themselves.

These complexes interfere with setting our goals in life. Their influence can leave a mark on your attitude to yourself and on setting goals for many years.

HOW DO THESE FEARS RESTRICT OUR POTENTIAL?

We start a business and calculations suggest we will have some profit, but the complex of failure does not allow us to make a favorable decision for our life. We refuse to carry out this project because of fear that our business may fail.

Fear of criticism: we stop dreaming, getting ideas, thinking positive, but dreams lead us to deeds, achievements, setting goals and achieving them. Your unique gift will initially exist only in your dreams. Dreams are extremely important in order to achieve our goals.

We dream, and then bring dreams to life; this is how it is conceived to be in the universe. When we stop dreaming, we have nothing to put into practice, we do not get positive ideas and life becomes gray and common. As a result, we do not set goals and do not bring our dreams to life.

Through acknowledging that mistakes are an integral part of the training, a person can break the vicious circle. The Great

Edison had suffered defeat ten thousand times before he made the incandescent bulb that gave light. Do not despair and do not give up if you fail once or twice before your plans start working!

THE POSITIVE EFFECTS OF CRITICISM:

1. It teaches us to control emotions. You do not get along in society if you have not learned to control and correctly show your emotions. You need to practice this skill.

2. It forces us to use reason and logic. Example: a person is accused of having promised to come at 10:00 but did not come on time. There might be good reasons why he could not do it, but instead of emotional reactions, one needs to be able to calm down and explain what happened. Because of criticism, we have to use our brain to build logical arguments — to present facts without emotion.

3. It shows the skeletons hidden in the closets. For many of us, there are areas in life, which we prefer to turn a blind eye on or just do not want to know more about it. And if some shrewd man reveals a secret, it helps a sincere and honest man to start to work on himself. If a person is offended, it means that he does not have peace with others and with himself.

4. It helps achieve emotional stability. If a person is able to maintain composure when he is criticized, scolded or corrected, it will help him in other areas of life. Exposure, self-control, control of one's emotions, these traits are useful everywhere: at home and at work. But if a person does not know how to deal with criticism, his life will be in chaos only because of the fact that the man has not learned to control himself.

5. Get rid of the wrong stereotypes. Example 1: someone thinks that if parents punish him, it means that they do not love him. Example 2: Many parents believe that children need to be spoiled, forgetting that then it can bring new problems. Criticism can help to get rid of these stereotypes.

6. It helps to become sober and adequate. If people perceive criticism negatively or even cannot accept it at all, then it indicates a high degree of being spoiled. Being spoiled means a suggested wrong perception of oneself in the context of reality–exaggerated or untrue vision of oneself. Criticism can make a person face the reality like nothing else, and it makes a person stronger, more appropriate and more holistic.

7. It helps to become less categorical, which means:
   • to give other people the right to make mistakes;
   • to allow the existence of other opinions other than your own;
   • to treat people from the position of the presumption of innocence.

   Some people have this kind of attitude: "There are only two opinions: my opinion and the wrong opinion." Criticism helps to find out that it may be wrong.

8. The skill of humbling relieves stress. Science has proven that the skill to agree with one's imperfections relieves stress and tension; brings a sense of happiness, peace, balance, joy and satisfaction by oneself. Stress is an emotionally sharp feeling of the difference between the desired and the real, between what you would like to be and who you really are.

So, fear of criticism and fear of failure are some of the main obstacles to achieving our goals.

9. These complexes do not allow us to adequately assess ourselves, they distort our reality, and because of them, we do not see ourselves as the ones we were created — talented, spirited, courageous, persistent, creative and proactive.

10. They steal our energy, which our body releases for the achievement of objectives, and spend it on feelings like "I won't succeed, I do not have talent, people will think wrong about me, and they will treat me badly..." etc. And for us, it is very important to get rid of these complexes.

THE GOLDEN NUGGETS

1. Fear of criticism is stealing our energy which should be directed to the achievement of our goals.

2. Fear of criticism distorts proper perception of ourselves and leads us to low self-esteem. We find it difficult to answer correctly the question "Who am I?" because we do not see virtues in ourselves and often compare ourselves to others, and not in our favor.

3. Fear of criticism is stealing our energy which should be directed to the achievement of our goals. It distorts our identification; we do not correctly answer the question: "Who am I?"

4. Fear of failure does not allow us to make decisions quickly, we are not proactive and therefore opportunities go past us without our using them.

5. Because of our feelings about the possible failure, we lose the energy which is intended for the fulfillment of our goals. And consequently, we cannot effectively complete our tasks.

SELF-EXAMINATION TEST

1. **Are you afraid of responsibility?**
   a) I do not like to take responsibility (0)
   b) I try to defeat my own fear (1)
   c) I'm not afraid of responsibility (2)

2. **Do you find it hard to decide to take up a new business or change your current job for a more promising one?**
   a) Yes, it's all about me (0)
   b) I work on myself to defeat my fear (1)
   c) I am inclined to change, I like new things (2)

3. **Do you worry that you do not get something?**
   a) Yes, often (0)
   b) I try to change my thoughts (1)
   c) I do not worry but act instead (2)

4. **If your business has been criticized by most people close to you, will you continue going to your goal?**
   a) I cannot, I need the support of allies (0)
   b) With some difficulty, but I will move on (1)
   c) Criticism will not stop me (2)

5. **Are you trying to meet the expectations of society regarding you?**
   a) Yes, I try not to stand out from the crowd (0)
   b) I have my own opinion, but I find it hard to press it (1)
   c) I do not spend my efforts to meet the expectations of others (2)

6. **Do you find it hard to express your opinion aloud?**
   a) Yes, I find it easier to remain silent (0)

b) It is difficult, but I'm working on it (1)

c) No, it is not difficult (2)

Test Results

0–4 points — We are sorry but you have this complex. You find it hard to make decisions independently to start something new, for example, a business. You are better staying in your previous work than looking for a better position. You always need the approval of your actions on the part of others. With this way of thinking it is very difficult to achieve your goals and fulfill your mission.

5–9 points — You sometimes feel the influence of the complex. You can worry about your new beginnings, but you try to conquer feelings and think constructively. You find it hard to express your opinion, but you have it, and under pressure, you dare to speak out. You fight your fears, and you are going in the direction of victory.

9–12 points — We are happy for you! You are not affected by this negative complex and all your energy is used for the achievement of your goals.

Recommended reading

||||||||||||||||||||||||||||||||||||||||||||||||||||||||||||||||||||||||||||

For a more detailed study of this topic I recommend reading the book "Freedom from fear" by "The University of Life." The truths contained in that book will help you to become free from fear of failure and fear of criticism.

CHAPTER 15

DENIAL

DENIAL

Fear of denial is considered to be the main complex which prevents successful self-actualization of a personality, because the fear of denial prevents building a sound and mutually beneficial relations in society, without which no successful business, career, education, work or personal life is possible. The fear of denial implies:

- avoidance of professional activity that requires significant interpersonal contact because of fear of criticism, condemnation or denial;

- the unwillingness of a person to deal with people without being sure that they will like him;

- prevention of oneself in forming intimate relationships for fear of ridicule or refusal due to low self-esteem

- concerns about possible criticism or denial in social situations;

- stiffness in new social situations because of feelings of inadequacy;

- perception of oneself as a person socially inept, as an unpleasant person or "inferior" to others;

- deep reluctance to take risks or engage in new activities, as this may reinforce the sense of shame.

You can make a natural conclusion that fear of denial is a major obstacle to the achievement of goals and adequate self-identification. With the fear of denial, it is difficult for us to build sound relationships with people. We perceive the world as a hostile place and treat people with suspicion. Because of this, we miss opportunities and we have no relationships; it is difficult for us to build a team, because of the relationship we will build in it on the basis of control and not giving people the opportunity for self-actualization. Building relationships in society, accordingly, prevents the successful self-identification, as self-actualization and achievement of goals are impossible without building strong and mutually beneficial relationships. In the end, it is difficult for us to achieve our goals and fulfill our destination.

Denial spoils people's vision of life with lies that one can only be accepted and loved when one has achieved success in life. This is the lie that programs further human behavior. A person steps on the thorny path to that success, the image of which is different for everyone. As a result, this person spends his entire life on gaining fame, wealth or power. In the end, he is disappointed, as neither success nor power can bring satisfaction and especially not love. People with this complex tend not to find themselves and to fulfill their purpose, but to achieve a certain status instead. Because of this, they cannot fulfill their life mission.

Achieving wealth and success does not lead to healing your inner wounds and complexes which you received in your childhood.

On the contrary, achieving the status that leads to permissiveness will affect you in the first place because an undeveloped person with wounds unhealed will manifest themselves in despotism, the desire to control everything that will turn the life of the wounded man and others who depend on him into a hell. Such a person finds it extremely difficult to achieve goals or realize his life mission because even understanding it, he may fail due to incorrect, distorted beliefs about himself, the world and other people in it.

As an example, I want to cite the story of a well-known TV host, Oprah Winfrey.

Every day approximately fourteen million viewers tune in to watch the "Oprah Winfrey Show" which is 55 percent more viewers than its nearest competitor. Ninety-nine percent of homes in America and in sixty-four countries of the world listen to it and watch it and thus ensure the annual income of $170million.

The early part of Winfrey's life was a continuous severe trauma and crisis. She was an illegitimate child abandoned by both parents. During her stay in a Milwaukee ghetto, she was raped at the age of 9 by one of her relatives, and then constantly sexually harassed by two other relatives.

And yet the impression is that these experiences have had a positive impact on Winfrey, prompting her to great heights. They helped her to manifest her super ability to learn which occurs in such traumatic situations.

This led Winfrey into a state when she had to tell herself: "I will overcome everything and be the best that I can ever be" and really she was that way, she felt her dignity and overcame the feelings of guilt and shame for abuse.

Yet already having achieved huge fame and success, Oprah attempted suicide. The reason was a prolonged depression because of her excess weight and inability to break bad relationships with the opposite sex. We can say that the reason lies in her childhood, denial and inability to go through the process of mental healing. When both these factors coincided, it resulted in the lowest emotional point in her adult life.

It was the most serious stop in Oprah's life when having the success to which she aspired, she had to go back emotionally into childhood and go again through the pain hidden deep within her soul. It was as if the pain caught up with her and tried to bring her back.

As we can see, denial can push a person forward to overcome odds and to succeed. However, this does not mean that having achieved a status, fame, money and power that this person will be able to heal his emotional wounds. As a result, there is a danger that even having fulfilled his destiny, the man can fail and never achieve the goal due to the fact that there was no inner healing. This complex is his weakest point, and in order to avoid getting thrown out of the saddle on the way to his goal, he should strengthen this point.

When denial occurs to us, there is a series of negative emotions or feelings that may look like this:

- denial breeds loneliness, since the person is hiding from people, situations, feelings, and emotions;
- loneliness is followed by feelings of pity, which keeps him in the prison of concern about his problems;
- pity brings depression;
- depression can lead to despair and hopelessness.

Self-pity leads to passivity, tears, depression, and destruction of relationships with people and to isolation from society or suicide.

WHAT IS DENIAL BASED ON?

Denial is based on the lack of love. This occurs because of the lack of love and coldness of parents, due to the fact that parents compare their child with other children, and senior children jealous of their junior brothers or sisters. Jealousy may also appear in adulthood as a result of divorce or a breakup of relationships.

HOW DO WE UNDERSTAND UNCONDITIONAL LOVE?

It's when you love a child when he's good, he has good grades at school, he has washed dishes, and you love him when he stumbles, does bad things and does poorly at school. You always accept him, separating the bad things from the nature of the child. He acts wrong, but you still love him, even when he doesn't deserve your love.

WHAT ARE THE CHARACTERISTICS OF DENIAL?

1. One cannot receive and give love.

2. One is too conscious of the opinions of others if they do not approve of him, he cannot act in accordance with the decision he has taken and as a result, he does not reach his goal.

3. One cannot build strong relationships in the family, society, at work, and he will always test them for strength, he finds it hard to trust people. In the end, the inability to build relations on a mutually beneficial basis hinders achievement of goals.

4. Loneliness, frustration, depression. Being in such states leads us away from our purpose and life mission.

WHAT CAN YOU ADVISE A PERSON WHO WANTS TO GET RID OF DENIAL?

1. Forgive all of the explicit and alleged offenders because of the excessive sensitivity you will feel hurt.

2. Accept the fact that you are different from others in the same way as they are different from you, and you don't need their approval to be yourself.

3. Open up towards other people. Make efforts to build relationships. Take the first step, try to see in a person a potential ally instead of an offender.

4. Accept yourself and love yourself with a non-selfish love the way you love a part of Creation.

THE GOLDEN NUGGETS

1. Denial is based on the lack of love. It occurs because of the lack of love and coldness on the part of parents; it may also occur in adulthood as a result of divorce or a breakup of relationship.

2. People with this complex cannot receive and give love.

3. Being too sensitive to the opinions of others makes them, if they are not approved by others, to be unable to act in accordance with the decisions made, which results in failure to achieve the goal.

4. One cannot build strong relationships in the family, society, at work, and he will always test them for strength, he finds it hard to trust people. In the end the inability to build relations on a mutual beneficial basis hinders achievement of goals.

SELF-EXAMINATION TEST

1. **How difficult is it for you to forgive people?**
    a) Yes, it was hard for me to forgive someone who offended me (0)
    b) I am in the process of working on myself striving for forgiveness (1)
    c) It's easy to forgive and I just try not to be offended (2)

2. **How often do you build "walls" between yourself and other people?**
    a) If someone does not treat me with proper attention, is cold to me or critical of me, I immediately build a wall in our relationship (0)
    b) I try not to build walls, but it does not always happen my way (1)
    c) I don't build walls; I am pragmatic in my relationship (2)

3. **Did you worry over the last year about a breakup of a relationship, a divorce, or quarrels with best friends?**
    a) Yes (0)
    b) There were conflicts (1)
    c) Nothing serious happened (2)

4. **How often do you have relationship conflicts?**
    a) They are frequent (0)
    b) Sometimes (1)
    c) I try to build relationship on a mutually beneficial basis (2)

Test results

0–4 points — We are sorry, but you have this complex. You find it difficult to build relationships with others, you try to control everything, and often treat people suspiciously. With this mind-set, it will be extremely hard to achieve your goals and fulfill your destiny. You will miss opportunities because of the excessive suspiciousness.

5–9 points — You sometimes feel the influence of this complex. You are suspicious; you often have conflicts with people, but you are working on yourself, realizing that this complex prevents the achievement of your goals and the fulfillment of your destiny. So, you are on your way to success.

9–12 points — We are glad for you! You are not affected by this negative complex and all your energy is directed to the achievement of your goals.

PRACTICAL TASKS

1. Write a list of all your imaginary and real offenders, of all who have ever hurt you.

2. Decide to forgive them.

3. Write a list of people with whom you have a strained relationship, or you have "walls" in your relationship. Make a decision to restore a good relationship with them.

Recommended reading

||||||||||||||||||||||||||||||||||||||||||||||||||||||||||||||||||||||||||||||

For a more detail study of this topic, I recommend you to read the books "Don't touch me, it hurts" and "What is wrong with me?" by "The University of Life."

CHAPTER 16

LOW SELF-ESTEEM

LOW SELF-ESTEEM

WHAT MAKES A PERSON HAVE A LOW SELF-ESTEEM?

It is not possible to identify one cause of low self-esteem for everyone. You form your beliefs about yourself over a long period of time and this process is likely to be affected by a myriad of things from early childhood through adulthood.

Some factors that can contribute to low self-esteem include:

1. Difficult childhood experiences — negative experiences in childhood, such as bullying, difficult family relationships or having a hard time at school, can be particularly damaging for your self-esteem.

2. Difficult life events — difficult experiences as an adult, such as divorce, death, loss of job, etc. While all of these are common life happenings, several of these together in a short period of time can damage one's self-esteem.

3. A tendency or culture of negative thinking will significantly lower self-esteem.

4. Being in or around a group who is always negative or ridiculing of you may lower your self-esteem.

5. Negative thinking patterns — you may learn or develop thinking patterns that reinforce low self-esteem, such as constantly comparing yourself to others or developing high standards for yourself that you can't achieve.

6. Limited social interaction either through your own making or because you are discriminated against, can lead to a poor self-image.

A low self-esteem distorts our perception, especially of ourselves. People with a low self-esteem do not believe that they can find themselves in this life, they do not believe in the realization of their potential. So their identification of themselves is distorted. As a result, it is difficult and almost impossible for them to fulfill their mission in life. Anyone can get them to yield. They cannot firmly defend their opinion because they are not sure that it is correct. Their energy is consumed by the negative complex.

Therefore, it is difficult for them to achieve the set goals. They spend a tremendous amount of time and energy for the uneasy feelings about their identity, for the comparison of themselves with the other, more successful people.

They do not believe in their own power and do not see their opportunities. A low self-esteem prevents us from achieving goals and fulfilling the mission.

WHAT HELPS TO FORM AN ADEQUATE SELF-ESTEEM?

A human who is a confident person cannot have a low self-esteem. If you want to raise self- confidence in your child, bring him up in an atmosphere of love, acceptance, and respect for his decisions, actions and beliefs.

If you do not form a character in your child, he will be susceptible to peers' opinion, even if it is a negative opinion, he will do like the majority of people do, without thinking about his own life. This is how drugs, alcohol, and prostitution come to people's lives.

A person with a low self-esteem is used to only taking and never giving anything in return.

It is difficult for such a person to promote products, services, find clients and achieve success.

Naturally, it is difficult for him to achieve his goals. He has a distorted image of himself. He does not identify himself with his Creator, does not believe that he has any skills, talents, gifts, faith, perseverance, creativity, or a comprehensive view of the world.

Consequently, he cannot achieve his goals because there is a limit in his mind which he will never overcome.

He will think himself to be worse than his customers, will not invest his time in others, and will not give a professional assistance, advice, and friendly service.

IF WE HAVE A LOW SELF-ESTEEM, HOW CAN WE GET RID OF IT?

1. Write at least 50 points, for which you can respect yourself. For example, you cook well, you are a confident PC user, you are a goal-oriented person, you keep your word, you are scrupulous, honest, etc.

2. To act is a constant action and achieving a goal will help you to raise your self-esteem.

3. Learn how to make decisions quickly. When you make a decision, your body releases extra energy in order to realize it. So you become an enthusiast.

4. Never compare yourself with others. It takes your energy away and distracts you from the implementation of your plans and goals. As we can see, complexes and negative behaviors prevent us from self- actualization and achievement of our goals. Everyone who wants to

implement his destiny and achieve his goals just needs to get rid of the restricting beliefs and complexes, which they have learned from their family and acquired in the society.

In this book, we give a detailed description of possible complexes and restricting beliefs. Work on them, change your reactions, change your patterns of behavior and become free from restricting thoughts and complexes.

Get the freedom to effectively achieve your goals and fulfill your mission in life.

THE GOLDEN NUGGETS

1. Low self-esteem distorts our understanding, especially that of ourselves. People with low self-esteem do not believe that they find themselves in life and realize their potential.

2. As a result, it is difficult, almost impossible, for such a person to fulfill his mission in life. Anyone can make him yield. He cannot firmly defend his opinion because he is not sure that it is correct. His energy is consumed by the negative complex.

3. He spends a tremendous amount of time and energy on anxious feelings about his identity, on comparing himself with other more successful people. He does not believe in his own power and he does not see his opportunities.

4. Low self-esteem prevents us from achieving goals and fulfilling the mission.

SELF-EXAMINATION TEST

Exercise "Which step am I encountering?"

The purpose of the exercise is to help the participants to build an adequate self-esteem.

The participants are given a form with a ladder of 10 steps of self-esteem pictured in it.

The following instruction is given: *"Draw yourself on the step at which you think you are right now."*

TEST RESULTS

The steps of the adequate level of self-esteem are **6 and 7.** These are the steps that are a little above the middle and most people assign themselves to these steps.

Step 8 can also be classified as a level of the adequate self-esteem, although it is assumed that in this case, the self-esteem is a little too high.

Steps 9 and 10 correspond to overestimated self-esteem. Such steps are chosen by the people who think they are much better than others. They believe that their traits make them pretty close to being ideal.

Steps 4 and 5 are chosen by people who are not entirely satisfied with their current situation and their self-esteem is low.

Finally, **steps 1 to 3** is chosen by the people with very low self-esteem, or those who are in a state of crisis.

The fact is that the choice of their place in the ladder of self-esteem can be influenced not only by the formed life-long vision of themselves but also by the current mental state of a person before the test.

PRACTICAL TASK

Write at least 50 points, for which you can respect yourself. For example, you cook well, you are a confident PC user, you are goal-oriented person, you keep your word, you are scrupulous, honest etc.

Recommended reading

||||||||||||||||||||||||||||||||||||||||||||||||||||||||||||||||||||||||||||||

For a more detailed study of this topic I recommend you to read the book "Do not touch me, it hurts" and "What's wrong with me?" by "The University of Life."

CHAPTER 17

WHAT IS THE DIFFERENCE BETWEEN WINNERS AND LOSERS?

WHAT IS THE DIFFERENCE BETWEEN WINNERS AND LOSERS?

> *"Success is the ability to go from failure to failure without losing your enthusiasm."* (WINSTON CHURCHILL)

> *"Success is the ability to suffer one failure after another without losing the will to win."* (WINSTON CHURCHILL)

When you were born, your brain was free of any information like a new computer with an absolutely clean hard disk drive. Thinking switches on your computer and launches the "operating system" directing your life. Parents or people bringing you up were the main programmers, who installed a certain "operating system" into your brain.

If children are given will-to-win spirit, persistence, endurance, self-confidence, happiness, and gratitude from their parents, they will live their life with an expectation of victory.

However, if you have been given nervousness, fears, suspicion, and distrust, you will automatically behave like a loser and, as a result, you will not be able to achieve set goals.

We should learn to reveal distorted thoughts, beliefs or patterns of behavior and replace them with correct ideas and beliefs.

Think of the example with a computer virus. What happens even to the best computer when a virus gets into it and destroys its modern software?

Firstly, some parts of a computer stop functioning properly and this device loses speed of operation. At long last, the computer freezes and can even crash. The same happens to our mind. A complex is a sort of virus that deactivates our system. If you let them spread all over your system, they will be able to influence your ability to function properly as it happens to a computer.

On this account, you cannot be effective and you will not be able to reach your goals.

You should get to know how to discern your complexes and beliefs that put many obstacles in the way of achieving your purpose and promote a distorted perception of yourself.

Then you should replace this distorted mentality with positive thoughts and beliefs. Developing the gratitude in your mind and learning how to be satisfied with all things that you have and your true being at a current moment, is also very essential. I will cite some distorted ways of thinking below. Doctor David Burns, a well-known psychiatrist and the author of the book "How to feel better," described them in a very good way.

1. The habit of expecting the worst things to happen. (Pessimists)

This generally accepted and distorted way of thinking is observed in people with a fear of failure complex. There are some examples of it: "If something bad ever happens, it will certainly happen to me"; "My director did not give me a smile today, most likely he has a bad attitude towards my personality"; "My husband was late from work today, so he probably has a mistress." When you persistently think of such things you offer them an opportunity to become a prophecy. Imagining an unfavorable coincidence of circumstances, you unconsciously attract them into your life. On the contrary, start to expect something good to happen to you.

2. **The habit to draw negative conclusions.**

This type of thinking is common among people with a denial complex.

You wrongly assume to know what other people are thinking about without having any facts to confirm your point of view. For instance, you drop in at a café and see two of your best friends dining out without you. They notice you and start to whisper to each other. You automatically feel that they are criticizing you or talking about your deficiencies. However, the reality is completely different. Try to notice when you tend to draw premature conclusions. Start to expect the best behavior from the people around you.

3. **The negative filter.**

Such a person turns a deaf ear to positive information and does not see anything good around him. On the other hand, he has a good ear for negative information and remembers it extremely well. He is focused on negative things and lets positive impressions go past him.

4. **Conclusions built on emotions.**

A man with such a mentality sees his feelings as an absolute fact. If he is scared of something, he is sure something bad will happen to him. A sound person detaches his emotions from the actual state of affairs. He understands that he can have an influence on every situation with his faith, positive motivation, analysis and reasonable decision-making regardless of what he feels at the present moment. Change your thoughts into a more positive way.

> *"Negative thoughts are like birds — they will be always flying over your head but do not let them build a nest in your mind and heart!"* (FOLK WISDOM)

Perhaps these beliefs originate from your childhood, perhaps someone told you that achieving success is unreal for you, and having drawn negative conclusions from your previous experiences, you have convinced yourself that success is unreal without money and connections, which you do not have, so it means that you are not meant to be successful.

Unfortunately, this distorted mentality puts obstacles in the way of our advancement, achievement of goals and fulfilling your destination. These negative thoughts steal our energy and arouse unnecessary emotions inside us.

You should alter your restricted vision in order to become capable of making headway. A man becomes what he thinks about. Thoughts are material stuff.

Ordinary people think about their problems and they always complain and object to something; doing so they assign doom to themselves because this is how the law of defeat works.

Never regret things you cannot change in any life circumstances. This is a golden rule. Make a decision not to mourn over yourself in order not to become a sacrifice, a victim in life. Otherwise, it will bring you to a failure.

Decide you want to be content.

Decide not to concentrate on problems that are beyond your power to change.

Think of your decision and move forward.

Decide to never think of fears. Don't be afraid of anything, ever. Decide to never think of doubts.

HOW DO PROMINENT AND SUCCESSFUL PEOPLE THINK?

- Successful people only think about their targets.

- They set a goal for a day, a week, a year, and for an entire life. They refuse to think beyond the scope of their goals. They seem to be obsessed by their goals.

- Successful people concentrate their attention on their tasks while ordinary people think of problems.

- What is the difference between goals and tasks? A Goal is an expected final result and tasks are interim, steps. Goals consist of tasks. Tasks are meant to be steps towards your goals. Your goal is nothing more than illusion without tasks.

- Successful people are people of goals, they constantly think of new goals and tasks.

- Successful people are constantly thinking about solutions, ways and methods to solve a certain problem.

- How to find a solution? What solution to make in the current situation? They are always deep in thought about their goal. They are permanently looking for solutions to promote their set goals and tasks.

- To rest does not mean to switch your mind off. Certainly, a man should rest. Certainly, rest is extremely important, but you should plan your activities during rest as well as the time of rest in order to take all advantages of it and receive a blessing.

- If your goal is not going to become your life, everything else will be useless. We are all descendants of God and therefore we have something unique given by Him. We all have the seed of greatness. Everyone has a calling to be a leader in a definite sphere of activity: politics, education, medicine, art etc. Everyone should find his own field and work on it.

- Successful people constantly think of their plans.

- Do you have any plans?

- Prominent people reflect on their future, building their tomorrow today.

- Do you plan your future systematically? Let's take control of our lives and start to build it in accordance with our plans.

- Successful people are constantly thinking.

- Successful people always have a positive vision of life.

- They do not think of defeat. They do not picture something to be impossible. They do not take the word "no" as an answer. They are positively tuned in and they never give up.

- Great people permanently reflect on the improvement of their affairs. They have never been in a state of inactivity. They constantly work on improving themselves and doing everything more efficiently.

- Successful people concentrate their attention on actions.

- "Something must be done." They cannot forgive their idleness. They do not relax in their actions.

- Successful people think how to do everything better and faster.
- They are searching for a way to do everything better and with higher speed.

Having a winner's mentality, you will be able to achieve your goals effectively and quickly.

The mentality of a loser will hamper the progress of reaching your goals and fulfilling your life destination. Even having answered the question "Who am I?" you will have a lot of obstacles in the way of getting to your purpose on account of a loser's negative way of thinking. You should find out your weak points and change yourself, the way you think, in order to complete your mission and live a winner's life.

THE GOLDEN NUGGETS

1. You should learn to reveal distorted thoughts and beliefs or patterns of behavior and change them into correct points of view and beliefs.

2. You should alter your restricted vision in order to become capable of making headway.

3. Changing your beliefs or re-adjusting them you will be able to alter your way of living.

4. The mentality of a loser will hamper the progress of reaching your goals and fulfilling your life destination.

5. You should find out your weak points in order to complete your mission and live a winner's life.

SELF-EXAMINATION TEST

1. **Do you complain of your destiny when something goes wrong?**
   a) Yes, I often do it (0)
   b) I try to solve the problem (1)
   c) I do not waste my energy on complaints and solve all my problems at once as they occur (2)

2. **Do you consider work to be the best medicine?**
   a) No, I do not think so (0)
   b) Fun is fun, as I suppose, but there's the job waiting (1)
   c) I agree (2)

3. **Do you have any plans for a day, a month, or a year?**
   a) No, I don't (0)
   b) I have a plan for a day (1)
   c) I have both long-term and short-term plans (2)

4. **Do you plan your future systematically?**
   a) No, I do not think about such distant future (0)
   b) I have already drawn up some plans (1)
   c) Yes, I plan my future systematically (2)

5. **Ha ve you ever found yourself thinking about defeat or picturing something to be impossible?**
   a) Yes, very often (0)
   b) Sometimes I think so (1)
   c) I am always confident of victory (2)

TEST RESULTS

0–4 scores — We are sorry for your mentality of a failure. You should alter your way of thinking; give up reflecting on problems and take overcoming them to be your first consideration. You should be aware of the purpose of your life and reflect on it or on the ways to fulfill it. Thoughts about your goal will bring a feeling of optimism. The mentality of a failure will hamper the progress of reaching your goals. You must change your beliefs in order to fulfill your destination.

5–9 scores — Sometimes thoughts of failure and defeat occur to you. Keep on working on yourself in order to change your ordinary mentality into winner's mentality. You will achieve your goals easily only with such type of thinking.

9–12 scores — We are happy for you! You have the mentality of a winner. All your energy is spent on achieving set goals.

PRACTICAL TASKS

Determine specific features in which your failure mentality manifests itself.

Play the models of winner's behavior in your mind during 21 days.

Recommended reading

||||||||||||||||||||||||||||||||||||||||||||||||||||||||||||||||||||||||||||||||

I advise you to read the books "How to live a 100% life?" and "Life is an opportunity" by "The University of Life" in order to study this topic better.

TEST: DO YOU HAVE AN INFERIORITY COMPLEX?

To complete this test, we suggest using the method of J. Manaster and R. Corsini (1982).

Here is its entire description:

You have 5 lines in front of you; each of them is presented as a continued scale. If you want, you can mark your scores on them. It will be your self-appraisal in comparison with other people, the same people as you are. For example, you are a white unmarried woman of 30 with a level of income. You will be appraising yourself compared to other women of the same race, age, and condition as you perceive them.

You should mark your score on the line; the score you choose relates to your general satisfaction by yourself. If you consider yourself to be a successful common person of a medium level, you may choose the score of 50%; if you see yourself at a level lower than medium, you may choose the score of 40, 35, 25 or even less; if you see yourself as a failure, you may use the score of 5% or 10%; if you have a good feeling of your personality and you seem to be a happy person, you may choose the score of 75%, 85% or 95%.

We suggest that you assign five marks.

1. Estimate the general success of yourself as a person in comparison with other people of the same group where you belong.

2. In the second scale, mark how other people appraise you, in your opinion. For instance, it seems to you that you

have 50%, but you think that people who know you may give you the score of 70%.

3. Now, please, give a mark to your hypothetical absolute maximum on condition if you had all opportunities and means needed to attain your goals.

4. Then rate yourself in the future. To your mind, what self-appraisal will you have in five years?

5. Finally, mark the point where you would like to be right now. What point should be yours?

Draw five vertical lines on a sheet of paper and mark these five points on each of them. Below, we will explain how to identify whether you have a tendency for an inferiority complex. Now we ask you to conduct self-appraisal because it tells you something about your own personality.

It will take a minute or even less, but you should do it on a piece of paper. If you do it only in your mind, it will not be enough.

TEST KEY

The level of inferiority complex is derived from the quantity of discrepancy between your marks in the first scale ("How do you assess yourself in general?") and the fifth scale ("Where do you want to be?").

If you assess yourself at **50%** and you are willing to be at the level of **60%**, this "small difference" will probably mean that you have a slight inferiority complex. However, if you grade yourself at **30%** and you are eager to have **100%**, you will obviously have a strong feeling of personal inferiority.

If having completed the test you turned out to have an inferiority complex you should analyze yourself and understand which particular complex steals your energy.

Above, we have described in details which complex you can suffer from: the feeling of guilt, victim complex, and fear of failure, criticism, poverty, loneliness and loss of love or success, lack of confidence, isolation, and low self-esteem.

Having realized your negative model of conduct, you will be able to reprogram your consciousness with a goal in mind and create a new model of conduct that will help you to promote self-actualization. Based on SELF-APPRAISAL SCALE (after Manaster C. J., Corsini R.J., 1982).

EPILOGUE

EPILOGUE

So, dear reader, we have reached the end of our journey. The greatest expectation derived from this book is your starting to be sure of changing your previous life and not finishing it in emptiness and disillusionment.

This book contains the instructions to learn so you will be able to change your life for the better, live a bright, interesting, unique, and rich life full of passion, pursuit, fulfillment, adventures, and discoveries. This book is written in order to prevent you from wasting your life on doubts and fears, in order to encourage you to establish yourself as a human being and Lord of Creation, in order to make your inimitable, beautiful, brilliant soul reveal itself. Live in accordance to what you have in your heart; don't lock your gift inside, step over limits and restrictions. There are no boundaries for your self-actualization, there are no limits for your gift that will pave the way for you and help you to be prominent, respected and successful.

You must do just a few things for that:

1. Answer the five major philosophical questions:

   - Who am I?
   - What can I do?
   - Why am I here?
   - What am I doing here?
   - Where am I going?

2. You must always be in active consciousness; you must always be here and now.

3. You must consciously build a system of values and beliefs.

4. You must research the topic you are interested in or your favorite activity. You must investigate this issue from all possible sides and find the maximum of information about it.

5. You must design a system that will turn your dream into reality.

6. Draw up a plan concerning your life target and destination and give detailed information about things which must be done every day accordingly to your purpose and life mission.

   Remember! A man will waste his day if he has not done anything connected with his goals and destiny.

7. You must break your purpose into the least measurable pieces i.e. days in order to know your field of everyday activity.

8. You must write down your goals and plans.

9. You must get rid of limited and negative beliefs.

10. You must break free from complexes that prevent you from fulfilling your destiny.

11. You must show your persistence, perseverance, and endurance on the path leading to your goal and destiny.

"Twenty years from now you will be more disappointed by the things that you didn't do than by the ones you did. So throw off the bow lines. Sail away from the safe harbor. Catch the fair winds in your sails. Explore! Dream! Discover!" (MARK TWAIN)

ABOUT PASTOR SUNDAY ADELAJA

Sunday Adelaja is the founder and senior pastor of the Embassy of God in Kiev Ukraine and the author of more than 300 books which are translated in several languages including Chinese, German, French, Arabic, etc.

A fatherless child from a 40 hut village in Nigeria, Sunday was recruited by communist Russia to ignite a revolution, instead he was saved just before leaving for the USSR where he secretly trained himself in the Bible while earning a Master's degree in journalism. By age thirty-three he had built the largest church in Europe.

Today, his church in Kiev has planted over a thousand daughter churches in over fifty countries of the world. Right now they plant four new churches every week. He is known to be the only person in the world pastoring a cross cultural church where 99% of his twenty five thousand members are white Caucasians.

His work has been widely reported by world media outlets like Washington Post, The wall street Journal, Forbes, New York times, Associated Press, Reuters, CNN, BBC, German, Dutch, French National television, etc.

Pastor Sunday had the opportunity to speak on a number of occasions in the United Nations. In 2007 he had the rare privilege of opening the United States Senate with prayers. He has spoken in the Israeli Knesset and the Japanese parliament along with several other countries. Pastor Sunday is known as an expert in national transformation through biblical principles and values.

Pastor Sunday is happily married to his "princess' Pastor Bose Adelaja. They are blessed with three children, Perez, Zoe and Pearl.

FOLLOW SUNDAY ADELAJA
ON SOCIAL MEDIA

Subscribe And Read Pastor Sunday's Blog:
www.sundayadelajablog.com

Follow These Links And Listen To Over 200 Of Pastor Sunday's Messages Free Of Charge:
http://sundayadelajablog.com/content/

Follow Pastor Sunday on Twitter:
www.twitter.com/official_pastor

Join Pastor Sunday's Facebook page to stay in touch:
www.facebook.com/pastor.sunday.adelaja

Visit our websites for more information about Pastor Sunday's ministry:
http://www.godembassy.com
http://www.pastorsunday.com
http://sundayadelaja.de

CONTACT

For distribution or to order bulk copies of this book, please contact us:

USA
CORNERSTONE PUBLISHING
info@thecornerstonepublishers.com
+1 (516) 547-4999
www.thecornerstonepublishers.com

AFRICA
Sunday Adelaja Media Ltd.
Email: btawolana@hotmail.com
+2348187518530, +2348097721451,
+2348034093699.

LONDON, UK
Pastor Abraham Great
abrahamagreat@gmail.com
+447711399828, +44-1908538141

KIEV, UKRAINE
pa@godembassy.org
Mobile: +380674401958

BOOKS BY PASTOR SUNDAY ADELAJA

Churchshift: *Revolutionlize your faith, Church and life for the 21st Century.*

Money Won't Make you Rich: *God's Principles for True Wealth, Prosperity and Success.*

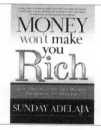

Time is Life: *History Makers Honor Time.*

Pastoring Without Tears: *It is possible to live and minister without sorrow and grief .*

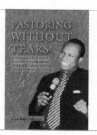

Olorunwa (There is God): *Portrait of Sunday Adelaja. THE ROADS OF LIFE.*

Made in the USA
Lexington, KY
11 April 2019